BLACK LEGACY PRESS™

WWW.BLACKLEGACYPRESS.ORG

Exploration of Aïr
Out of the world north of Nigeria
By
Angus Buchanan

Copyright © 2024 by BLACKLEGACYPRESS.ORG
All rights reserved. No part of this publication may be reproduced or transmitted in any form or by any means electronic or mechanical, including information storage and retrieval systems without permission in writing from the publisher, except for student research using the appropriate citations.

ISBN: 978-1-63652-419-1

EXPLORATION OF AÏR
OUT OF THE WORLD NORTH OF NIGERIA

ANGUS BUCHANAN

TO MY FATHER

A THOROUGH SPORTSMAN OF THE FINE OLD SCHOOL

PREFACE

A NARRATIVE of an odd undertaking to a foreign land. Odd, in the first place, insomuch that for the greater part of a year a man's tongue was mute to the language of his race, for the land where he travelled was native: first to the Hausa people; later to Hausa, Beri-Beri, Fulani and Tuareg; and later still to Tuareg alone; while over all there was a mere handful of French Europeans, who were the military administrators of law and order.

The country was that known as the Territoire Militaire du Niger of the Western Sudan, wherein, remote and in the midst of desolate seas of sand, lies the wild brooding mountain country of Aïr or Asben—which was the traveller's goal.

It might be said that the traveller was a rude man, for he was untutored in the deep studies of the scholar of many languages, as in a measure might be expected and understood of one whose occupation called him from day to day to don rough clothing and shoulder a rifle and march outside the frontiers of civilisation.

Clumsy, therefore, were his beginnings in speech with the people of the land; clumsy also his studies and understanding of all things new and strange which unfolded before his eyes in that amazing succession of novelty that taxes a balanced capacity of observation when one stands spell-bound at the entrance of an unexpected wonderland. Nevertheless, day by day, confusion became less; small words came of many tongues; piece by piece threads of understanding became woven into something durable and of the character of trustworthiness.

So that to-day I—for, alas, I must use that personal pronoun which is hateful to me, and admit that I am the traveller, so that I may shoulder the full responsibility as to the faithfulness of this narrative—have taken courage to tell my story with all its shortcomings, but at the same time with an earnestness that may in the end reveal, perhaps, the greater part of the picture of a strange land as it appeared to me.

And I would tell you that it is a wholly pleasant task to sit at home—*Home*, with all its repose and sweetness, neither sun-exhausted nor limb-weary, and with a full repast at hand—and look backward on the trail through the Sahara, and hear in imagination the fierce wind that brings a blinding sandstorm on its billows, and only have to write about it all.

But, though thus it is to-day, to-morrow or the day after I may be gone once again to the uttermost corners of the world—for such is my calling.

Some of my countrymen might envy me my to-morrow, some might pity me; but to all I would say neither one thing nor another. Such adventurings have their rare hours of pleasure and excitement and their long weary periods of trial and endurance. He is wise who knows the hazard of life stripped of all its romance and does not expect to find either great compensation or great gladness in strange lone lands—in the same way as they are seldom to be found in any man's labours of the common-place day.

It is deep satisfaction to me to know that, so far as the collections brought back are concerned, my labours have not been in vain, for it is one of my greatest desires, and the desire, I am sure, of many loyal-hearted men, to see Great Britain ever striving to continue to hold the honourable and prominent place in the development of the Natural History of the World which she has held in the Past. A year or two ago there were numerous and able rivals in the field, and Germany and America appeared to be on the verge of leading the world in all scientific research. Though a set-back to the former has occurred through the unfortunate circumstance of war, rivalry of nations will undoubtedly continue in the labyrinths of research, and, I trust, will be welcomed from any quarter as a healthy element that will ever give incentive to the students and scientific workers of this country to hold their own, and offer inducement to public-spirited people to encourage and support their commendable efforts.

The humble work, which in the following pages I venture upon, is not in any way a treatise on Natural History, but is a narrative descriptive of strange scenes and peoples in Out-of-the-World places in which Aïr has prominent position. And Aïr, in the centre of the Sahara, is unknown, or virtually unknown to English-speaking people. The German explorer Dr. Barth, in his travels in Central Africa, 70 years ago (1850-1), on behalf of the British Government, passed through Aïr, and in his *Travels in Central Africa* gave some brief discursive description of the country, which is, so far as I am aware, the only account of Aïr that we have in modern English literature.

But to return to my first remark, there are other reasons than that given in the first place for terming this an odd undertaking, and they are that the journey, which totalled some 1,400 miles of camel-travel, led to a land that was almost virgin to exploration of any kind, and of which nothing was known; while by force of circumstances it was decided for me that I must go on my long journey alone if I wished to undertake it; and therefore, perforce, I set out without the two or three good comrades that can help so greatly to lighten burdens, real or imaginary, on long uncertain trails.

The primary object of the Expedition, which was undertaken in the interests of the Right Honourable Lord Rothschild, was to link up the chain of Zoological Geography across that portion of Central Africa which lies between Algeria in Northern Africa and Nigeria in West Africa. Previous research had advanced from the south as far afield as Kano in Nigeria, and from the north to the Ahaggar Mountains in the Sudan southwest of Fezzan. There remained a great intermediate space unexplored by naturalists, wherein are the French possessions known as the Territoire Militaire du Niger and the unsettled mountainous region of Aïr or Asben; and it was through those said countries that the expedition proposed to journey.

With regard to the term Aïr or Asben which is applied to the great range of mountains which lie north of the region of Damergou, I think it is a pity that there should exist the seeming doubt of correct designation which the double title implies, and for my own part I propose, through my narrative, to refer only to the country as Aïr, which is the correct name in the language of the Tuaregs who inhabit the region, whereas Asben is a Hausa name, and would appear to have no particular claim to recognition since it is not Hausa country in the present era, whatever it may have been in the distant past, when tribal and religious wars were continually forcing territories to change hands.

The altitude readings, which I note during the narrative, since many of them have not been previously recorded, were taken with an aneroid barometer set to sea level before starting on the expedition.

Although the expedition was to a French colony, I feel that it was foreign only so far as concerned the difference of language, for the few officers I encountered, who so ably helped me on my way, if help I needed, were big-hearted men of the Lone Places among whom one could not feel a stranger. To all I owe thanks for such success as I gained, and gladly give it should any old comrade of the open road read this humble work.

I am indebted, also, to the administrative officials in charge of the Kano district who kindly rendered me many services ere I set out to cross the boundary.

Collecting in the field is one side of Natural History research, but there is, as you are aware, another side—the painstaking study of the specimens after they are unpacked on the museum benches at home. And I am much indebted to Lord Rothschild, Dr. Hartert, and the British Museum for having most kindly furnished me with the full results of the skilled studies of research to which the collections have been subjected since my return, for in so doing they have placed most valuable records at my disposal, so that I may draw from that large fund of knowledge when desired and enhance the value of this work.

ANGUS BUCHANAN.

CONTENTS

Introduction 1

CHAPTER I
Engaging Boys—Lagos 4

CHAPTER II
Kano, Northern Nigeria, The Commercial Metropolis Of The Western Sudan 15

CHAPTER III
Hausa, Currency, Camels, Travelling 34

CHAPTER IV
A Day's Work Collecting 58

CHAPTER V
Zinder 69

CHAPTER VI
The Shores Of Bushland And Desert 77

CHAPTER VII
Ostrich Hunting 89

CHAPTER VIII
Leaving The Bushland Behind: Aïr Entered 113

CHAPTER IX
Agades 126

CHAPTER X
Aïr: North To Baguezan Mountains And Hunting
Barbary Sheep...139

CHAPTER XI
In Baguezan Mountains..154

CHAPTER XII
The Northern Regions Of Aïr: Part I 167

CHAPTER XIII
The Northern Regions Of Aïr: Part Ii 185

CHAPTER XIV
East Of Baguezan, Aouderas, And Tarrouaji....................................202

CHAPTER XV
The Tuaregs Of Aïr 217

CHAPTER XVI
Heading For Home...226

Appendix 233

Footnotes 243

INTRODUCTION

Ever since Dr. Hartert[1] came to Tring, twenty-nine years ago, I have been keenly interested in the isolated mountains of Asben or Aïr in the middle of the Sahara, and the country surrounding them. This was chiefly owing to Dr. Hartert's account of his interview with some Tuareg traders who had come down into Nigeria to sell salt. This interest was intensified by our own explorations in Algeria and "Les Territoires du Sud," and Geyr von Schweppenburg and Spatz's journeys in the Ahaggar Mountains, all of which yielded many zoological treasures. Therefore, Dr. Hartert and I felt much satisfaction when, after his strenuous labours in the war in East Africa, Captain Angus Buchanan fell in with our views and undertook to explore Asben and the country between it and Kano, in North Nigeria, the terminus of the new railway. The eleven months occupied in the undertaking have proved most fruitful, for, besides the interesting ethnological and other facts recorded in the subsequent pages of this book, the zoological results have been most valuable. These latter results have been published in *Novitates Zoologicæ*, the journal of the Tring Museum, in a series of articles by Messrs. O. Thomas and M. A. C. Hinton,[2] Dr. Hartert and myself.

The number of new species and sub-species is very large, especially among the Mammals; Mr. Thomas indeed says that he has never known a collection of Mammals, from a limited area such as this, with so large a proportion of novelties. Among the new Mammals, the most interesting are undoubtedly the "Gundi" (*Massoutiera*), the Rock-Dassy (*Procavia*), and the "Mouflon" (*Ammotragus*), because of the immense stretches of desert which separate them from allied species and sub-species.

Among the Birds, one of the most interesting is the beautiful goatsucker (*Caprimulgus eximius simplicior*), for, although a slightly different subspecies, it illustrates once more the fact that many species inhabit a belt south of the Sahara from N.E. Africa across the African Continent to West Africa, while most of the forms north and south of that belt do not show such a wide range from east to west.

Among the Lepidoptera, the most interesting species are all true "desert" forms, with a wide range reaching through Arabia into India, although several new species and sub-species of butterflies and moths of great interest are also in the collection.

From a zoo-geographical point of view the collection is most valuable, for we now know zoologically a complete section of the "Great Saharan Desert," with the exception of the small portion between the Ahaggar Mountains and Asben, and although the region of the Sahara south of the former is undoubtedly tropical, and not palæarctic, in its fauna, it is very remarkable what a large number of palæarctic species and genera are still to be found there. Unlike most of the collecting-grounds of the Old World, which can still yield new and undescribed forms, Asben and its neighbourhood were absolutely virgin soil zoologically, and Captain Buchanan's specimens are the first to reach the hands of scientific workers. Considering the long journey by camel and the fact that Captain Buchanan was working absolutely single-handed, the collecting of over 1,100 Birds and Mammals and over 2,000 Lepidoptera, in a region notorious for its paucity, both of species and individuals, is a remarkable achievement, and proves him to be a most efficient explorer and naturalist.

ROTHSCHILD.

TRING MUSEUM,
March 22nd, 1921.

CHAPTER I
ENGAGING BOYS—LAGOS

It was at Seccondee on the Gold Coast that "John" came aboard. Do not mistake me!—he was not a first-class passenger nor an acquaintance. Far from it; he was one of a motley crowd of jabbering natives which, with an extraordinary conglomeration of hand-carried household belongings, were put aboard from surf boats and herded on to the open after-deck—already stacked with sacks of Kola nuts from Sierra Leone—like so many head of frightened sheep.

No! John was certainly not of a race or rank to claim intimate acquaintance. In the first place he was as black as the ace of spades, which in itself for ever barred him from any claim to equality or kinship—a hard plain fact which any old colonial on "The Coast" or anywhere in Africa would endorse, while with grave misgivings regretting the extraordinary policy and laws that grow, from what sane source is past understanding, more and more lenient in their evident stiffness of opinion to release native inhabitants of our colonies from the slightest restraint of a dominant European rulership; policy that is reacting— surely not with short-sighted blindness?—to bring about the downfall of the fine old decorum of the white man's prestige which natives naturally observed in every respect in the past. And it would be well to remember, those singular innovations which are being brought in on the tide of European civilisation are being entrusted to natives who are endowed by nature with characteristics of a different race type to ours and which are irrevocably unchangeable at the line of their limitations. European education and European laws along certain well-chosen, sure-set lines can cultivate those characteristics of the native to a certain standard—*but not one step further*. It is the logic of Nature: up to a point, with many creatures and plants and even matter, artificial cultivation is possible and beneficial; but over-experiment with the material, over-nurture and Nature steps in and calls a decisive halt in this tampering with her creations, and death or decline is thenceforth observed.

It is difficult for anyone to foresee the Future— that word of wonderful depth which is the most awesome in the English language—into which men may cast the biggest venturings of experiment in the world; and generations watch them rise and flourish if they be right, or flounder and go under if they be wrong. And surely it shall never be— this would-be blending of two entirely opposite races to a semblance of equality, though it is for the present this ugly threat which is often before the "Coaster" and the men on the bush stations to-day.

But to return to John, for John has importance in the narrative, which African politics have not, the ship had hauled anchor and cleared Seccondee for Lagos, and I stood solitary by the taffrail of the upper deck looking idly on the low line of typical African shore that lay indistinctly in the north. The deck, for the moment, was free of passengers, for it was in the quiet afternoon hours, when almost everyone on board retired to indulge in a pleasant book or a snooze, as is the after-lunch habit in hot enervating climates like Africa.

But, suddenly, I was not alone, and a native, who had no doubt watched his chance to break the bounds of the lower-deck, stood beside me waiting permission to speak.

"What do you want?" I asked, somewhat curiously. "You have no right to be on this deck."

"I want I make work for you, sir," replied the native. "My massa, he live for back, him go England. I plenty glad work for you, sir."

"But," I warned, "suppose I want a boy? I am a hunter. I am not going to live in a town or station in Nigeria where the duties of cook-boy or house-boy are ordinary. I am going to travel far in a strange land north of Kano; work will be hard and plenty; good boys will catch good pay; bad boys will go home quick and catch nothing. You are a coast boy, and I do not think you are fit for bush in far country."

But the boy was not so easily discouraged, either he wanted employment urgently or was ignorant of the full purport of my "white man talk," for he answered in his pigeon English, with a broad grin of hopefulness: "Dat be all same same, sir! I no fit savvy dat bush now, dat's true, by-n-bye I plenty fit to look him. I want work for you—I good boy, sir!"

To which what could one do but smile? But, nevertheless, I now looked the boy over more attentively.

His thick-set bulldog head was excessively ugly and unprepossessing in all its features. Any face is dull which has no attraction in the eyes or in the mouth, and those of this negro native had none, for the soiled whites of his eyes rolled alarmingly, and the large mouth had lips rolled into one that would have served three ordinary men adequately. Moreover, he was an Awori native of the Coast, and had profuse tribe marks on his face: three small deep-stamped marks over the cheek-bones, and a line of fourteen marks of the same stamp between the eye-corners and ears, while on the centre of the forehead he had a sort of square and compass scroll more lightly branded than the rest. He was clad, not in the picturesque nakedness of the aboriginal, but, after the fashion of the majority of "boys" on the Coast, in the cast-off clothing of some late master—even to a tweed cap, which sat with ridiculous incongruity on his black woolly head. Altogether he was a regular dandy in "rig-out." But he was no exception in that respect, for the comical and audacious dress of house-boys of his kind, who are inordinately full of personal swagger, has ever been a source of much amusement to colonials and strangers alike.

It did not take long to size the native up and note those brief somewhat unfavourable characteristics. But at the same time I had appraised the thick-set, sturdy build of the boy, so that the conclusions I finally arrived at were: "An ugly devil—not over intelligent, no doubt—but strong and healthy, and should stand up through plenty of hard work—and he looks honest."

"What's your name?" I asked.

"John, sir!" he replied. "John Egbuna," he added, by way of giving his full name; for it was no less a person than he who had come aboard at Seccondee.

"All right," I said, moving towards the deck smoking-room. "Come to me when we dock at Lagos and you can work for me."

Thus John made his appearance. By keen watchfulness he had risked the abuse of ship's officers and stolen a chance interview, and taking him on in this way was a chance shot, but time proved it to be a lucky one, for John went right through the whole expedition, ever faithful as a dog to his master, while his companions, one by one, fell out.

The ship docked at Lagos after she had come in over the bar

on an early morning tide, and steamed slowly inshore and up the wide river-like tidal lagoon of muddy water disfigured with surface-floating green slime-like vegetation and white froth, which escaped, no doubt, from some swamp bank further inland. It was a lagoon which was nevertheless picturesque and novel, with a light morning haze upon waters from which protruded the poles and loosely hanging nets of many fish traps, past which, or about which, up and down the lagoon, plied long lithe dug-outs, and odd-shaped craft of many kinds, single-sailed, or pole-driven, or paddled, and paintless and dark as their negro occupants, except where the gay colour of a cotton garb caught the eye on a boatman more extravagant than his brethren, who were generally rag-clad or naked to the waist.

At Lagos, when I had landed, I made the disconcerting discovery that there was no hotel—a circumstance strange in a port of importance and modern in nearly every other way. I had natives to engage in Lagos for my forthcoming travels, and other business, and therefore it was necessary to stay a few days in the place. Lagos, being a crowded town, was not the sort of place one could pitch a tent in, or that would have been quickly done; but I finally overcame the difficulty by interviewing the purser on the ship, who kindly allowed me to retain my berth on board while the ship unloaded her cargo.

And in that little cabin, in the course of events, some strange interviews were entered on. I had an old-country friend on shore, and with true Coast courtesy he sent his head-boy out into the native town to carry the news that there was a white man on the ship who wanted natives to go north with him, but that, "he want to look boy fit to skin fine fine."

Native news travels fast even in modern Lagos, and soon

boys of various races and types began to come aboard armed with their pass-books and letters testifying character—in some cases letters which were truly from past masters, in others, false and flattering documents borrowed for the occasion were tendered, such is the unscrupulous craftiness of some castes.

The outcome of two days of interviewing natives was not very encouraging, since no boy was discovered who could skin birds or animals with practical skill. However, at the end of the second day I had selected three boys and dismissed the rest, despite their clamourings to be heard further and reluctance to leave the ship.

One of the natives held over for further examination was an extraordinary individual, with all smooth face features absolutely obliterated by the mass of seared vertical lines of tribe marks which ornamented his entire face. He was of middle age, lean, and hard-looking, and obviously the hunter and tracker that he claimed to be. What this individual proposed, when an engagement was broached, was that he be allowed to go to his tribe in the first place to take the news of his departure to his people, and then return and catch up with my caravan wherever I might be. Inquiry revealed that his home was distant a whole month's travel by canoe along the coast. It would take him two months to go and return, and after that he would have to find my camp "somewhere" north of Kano. Yet he appeared to think nothing of such distance and to take to travelling as a duck to water, and declared with conviction that he would meet "master" anywhere, if he would but employ him. I had met this type of tireless hunter among natives before, and they are invariably very good if you can secure them. But, all things considered, taking the man on in faith of fulfilment of merely verbal promises, and advancing him some money to provide for his wives in his absence, savoured too much of bad business; and as he would not pack up and come along as he stood, he was finally allowed to go, with the understanding that if he hurried to his tribe and caught up with the expedition north of Kano, he would then be taken on at good wages, and his "back-time" made good.[3]

The other two boys were Hausa natives, the tribe that I had been strongly advised by men of experience to get my boys from if possible. They were both young—20 to 23—and had been selected from the crowd as being in appearance the most intelligent, for as it was of the utmost importance to secure some help in dressing specimens in the field, it was my intention to teach them to skin if in early practice they should show any aptitude for the work.

Hence one of them was sent ashore to the market in Lagos with instructions to buy a pair of tame pigeons, which would suffice for my purpose in lieu of a specimen dropped to the gun.

Thereafter, down in the hot narrow cabin, while the ship lay at anchor, I gave an object lesson on bird skinning—a necessary but not very edifying proceeding. To begin with, there was a ridiculous familiar pillow-cushion aspect about those dead *tame* pigeons which robbed one at once of any æsthetic enthusiasm, no matter how solemnly I was prepared to set about the delicate operation of skinning; and a glance from the work-table to my pupils, great loutish curly-headed negroes, with no appreciable sign of dawning understanding as my handiwork proceeded, made me much more inclined to laugh than to be serious.

When the lesson for the day was over, I sent the boys home with money to buy each a pigeon, which they were to try to skin in their homes in the way I had shown, and bring their handiwork on the morrow.

In due course they came aboard again with their "specimens": one poor skin in rags and with half the plumage gone, the other not so heavily handled, and showing some signs of painstaking work. On that day the lesson in my cabin was repeated, and then independently at home, and the result was that, on the eve of starting north to Kano, one boy—Sakari by name—was engaged, since he had shown some intelligence and skill over his skinning lessons, and the other dismissed as useless, as he had developed no aptitude for the work.

It may not be out of place to say here, while on the subject, that in spite of reports one hears at times of natives who have become expert at preparing specimens—doubtless exceptions—I would advise no collector to rely on local skill to any great extent, for I have always found them most difficult to educate, and skilful and careful only up to a certain point. For my own part I have never employed a native on such work who, when the skin was separated from the carcass, I could allow to apply the coating of preservative and reset the specimen in the natural, faultless repose which is essential to a finished skin required for scientific purposes. For straightforward skinning, however, good natives are procurable, and with practice can save much of the collector's time by doing the preliminary work.

Meantime, while hunting preparations were progressing, I had spent some time on shore each day in the native quarters of Lagos. The port at which a traveller disembarks in a land which is foreign always holds the lively interest of novelty, if nothing more, and Lagos had much that was novel. Notwithstanding the fact that the outward aspect from the lagoon is almost entirely

European, Lagos is, broadly speaking, a great native city; and it is on that account that it is so attractive to the curious stranger. The European section, which runs chiefly in a line along the long shores of the lagoon, is as a rampart between the sea and the great area of native town which lies hidden behind the solidity and imposing stature of the commercial and domestic buildings of the white man. And it is behind those colonial buildings that one must pass to gain entrance to the true city of primitive native hutments which bears the aspect of the historic antiquity and primitive character of the people who inhabit it. So turning from the main street which runs along the water-front, and walking up one of the side-streets, one finds oneself immediately among curious scenes and curious people in narrow streets which are lined with irregular closely packed native huts on either side— huts of every imaginable shape, and built, for the most part, with a most nondescript collection of materials which owners appear to have gathered together with little or no cost to their pockets. The walls of the huts are of mud, but the roofs, if they are not thatched, and the little dog-kennels of bazaars which are in front of almost every dwelling, are made up with old crate-boards, planks, corrugated iron, pieces of tin, old sacks, canvas— anything; paintless, untidy squalor for the most part, and the sun-basking places of countless lizards that come out from behind the shady cracks.

Were the huts and the streets deserted of human life, Lagos would indeed be a dismal place, and little short of one huge rubbish heap; but it is entirely otherwise, for the scene is crowded— even overcrowded—with life and colour, and hence attractive and sometimes very beautiful, and down the hot dusty streets, which in many instances are very narrow, and in and out of side lanes, one may pass for hours and never be clear of the brilliant cotton-clad throng; every individual of which, whether Yuroba, Egba, Hausa, Arab or Kroo, seems intent on selling or buying something in a veritable hive of trading and industry.

It is an uncommon sight, and a wonderfully picturesque one, to view those busy streets of native Lagos—their fullness of motion and rich, almost Oriental colouring of native dress, worn as a rule with all the grace of perfect physique; bazaars bright with wares exposed for sale; children toddling by the doors; and goats and chickens, at risk of their lives, tripping and feeding among the throng. Time without number, as I passed curiously through those streets, my eye was arrested by little gleams of perfect colouring in a perfect natural native setting—lovely pictures without one single act of preparation or posture—and I confess I sighed and moved on, regretting I was not an artist with genius to catch such scenes, and hold them in all their beauty and simplicity, so that I might show them also to my fellow-men, less fortunate in their freedom to travel.

Wherefrom it may be gathered that I much enjoyed my brief sojourn in Lagos, where I would fain have stayed longer, had not my duties called me to hurry on to Kano.

THE AUTHOR.

VIEW OF KANO CITY.

CHAPTER II
KANO, NORTHERN NIGERIA, THE COMMERCIAL METROPOLIS OF THE WESTERN SUDAN

TWICE a week a mixed passenger train runs from Lagos to Kano, which, despite its crude discomfort, must serve the traveller who wishes to go north, for there is no other way for the present.

When the time came for me to set out upon that journey, to say I was astonished at the crowds of natives at the station and at the confusion would be to put it very mildly. Drowning the sound of clanking trucks and blasts of engine whistles in the station, arose the deafening cries of instruction and abuse of a highly excited, hustling mob about to board the train, after bidding demonstrative farewells to two or three generations of relations and friends. Din and confusion reigned supreme; there was no calm eddy there, no steady head or hand to order silence or orderliness. One might be forgiven if, for the moment, one thought, as I did, that I had mistaken my direction and had entered a native market-place, in which a great sale was going on and the bidding eager and heated, in a volcanic atmosphere of excitement.

Patience was necessary, I assure you, to carry master and boys and baggage through the jostling of some hundreds of people, past the ticket-desks of distracted native clerks, who were being overwhelmed by a fiercely gesticulating, clamouring mob, that know, by force of primitive environment, only their rude desires and nothing of manners. And when the train had finally been boarded and the journey begun, I found it was necessary to keep hold on patience throughout, for many stations on the way held something of the same fearful din and disorder.

Much could be done by strict measures on the part of the railway authorities to "tone down" and regulate such native shortcomings, which white men would surely welcome, for it is little less than unchecked raw exuberance that is prevalent among them—perfectly good-natured, as a rule—which interferes with the quick and systematic disposition of the service, and which is not in keeping with the fitness of things in modern travel.

But such circumstances are among the drawbacks which unprecedented prosperity has brought in its wake. Nigeria, rich beyond all possible estimate in natural resources, has come, and is coming, into her own; no longer gradually and steadily as cautious and perhaps wise men might wish, but by leaps and bounds in keeping with the impatient spirit of the age. So that laggards are apt to be left behind, or things which are primitive become out of date; and that is what has happened with the Nigerian railway, which was built, no doubt, and run for the little needs of the colony as they existed a few years ago, but which is not now an adequate nor well regulated service, and fails sadly to fall in line with the astonishing progress of present-day commerce. Hence, in part, the cause of the congestion and confusion at the stations which is so prevalent to-day.

Nigeria urgently needs more railways, more railway facilities, throughout the width and breadth of the land: a land that has few equals in untouched natural wealth; *a land of immense possibilities, provided wise laws conserve its native labour* and cease to over-educate and over-wean it, and bring it back to the natural conditions from which it has been swept in a whirlwind of haste to clutch Prosperity and let everything else go by the board. Meantime it is bottled up in its vast interior for lack of outlets, while it is struggling like a thing unborn to break loose from bondage.

It is only a very little of the awakening, of the struggling, which one sees at almost every station "up the line," but every sign, little or great, is a sure forecast of a dawning and, perhaps, wonderful new era in West Africa.

The three days' wearisome journey to Kano need not be dwelt on at length. Throughout it was through a country rich in forest and bush, with no great change in geographical aspect or in altitude. The change in appearance begins in the Kano region, at the end of the railway, where the sub-deserts of the north come down in places to the fringe of the bushland and grade one into the other. The elevation of Kano is 1,700 ft., and this comparatively small change in altitude over the long distance from the coast to Kano—a distance of 704 miles—takes place gradually, so that the country, with small exceptions, appears flat throughout. There are great dense belts of oil palms and coco-nut palms in from the coast, which in time, as you proceed up-country, give place to more varied tropical forests of tall stately trees growing from jungle undergrowth; while further on again, toward the north, the growth is less prolific, and there is much acacia bush, which is open or dense in patches, and of no imposing height.

To step from the train at Kano and shake oneself free from the discomforting heat and dust of the carriage and know that the journey was at an end was a cause for rejoicing with me. Civilisation now lay behind; here would I gather together my caravan of camels and natives and set out on the open road with all the freedom of a nomad.

And as a starting-off point, I learned, on close acquaintance, that Kano was ideal, for it proved to be a place of the frontiers and of the outdoors that harboured a host of wayfarers that passed to and fro from the great and historical market-centre of the north.

The ancient city of Kano is situated on an extensive plain of cleared and cultivated bushland, which is not completely bare and waste nor treeless, but which, nevertheless, bears a distinctive change from the country further south, and has much of the appearance of sub-desert in the dry season, for it holds the palest of colouring—that true buff shadeless neutral tint common to desert lands which oceans of wind-lain sand and ranges of dry prairie grass give to a sun-parched, rain-thirsty country. But only in colour and sand-winds of the Harmattan has it great resemblance to desert, for, beside the scattered trees and bush, the level stretches on closer inspection are found to be largely lands that have been cultivated during the short rainy season and are now waste-grown over a very sandy soil, which is dry and cracked and powdered to fine dustiness on the surface. One of the common and best-known ground plants amongst the dead vegetation on the sandy soil is that named "Tafasa" by the Hausa people (*Sesbania sp. Leguminosæ*). It is a straw-yellow, long-stalked underbrush, with long thin bean-pods, and known to everyone about Kano, for it grows about 2 ft. high in considerable extent, and crackles noisily in brittle dryness as one brushes against it in passing. Another well-known plant there, and everywhere in the bushland, is that which the natives call "Karengia" (*Pennisetum Cenchroides Rich.*), and which is a very annoying burr-grass that adheres to any part of one's clothing, and which is a terrible pest to the hunter.

It was the season of the Harmattan when I reached Kano, for it was the month of December, and the driving winds from the Sahara had already set in. The Harmattan (often designated "Hazo" by Hausa natives, which means mist) is a season of hot, dry, dust-filled winds that blow from the desert interior steadily day after day, but seldom with the abandoned fierceness of a sandstorm. At that period the early mornings are cool even to coldness, and fresh and vigorous with the stirring of strong wind, which bears down with the coming of day, and brings with it a fine mist-like haze which envelops the whole country. But the haze is not an atmosphere of laden dampness, such as is familiar to England; quite the contrary, for it is dry with the intensity of a white heat, and mist-like only because the wind is so full of fine sand particles from the tinder-dry desert in the north, which it carries and lays in a carpet of fine penetrating dust wherever it passes.

The dryness in the land at this season is unbelievable if you have not experienced it; moisture is dried up as if the flame of a furnace was licking at it; ink, for instance, dries as fast as each letter of the alphabet is penned, and the clogging pen-nib is almost unmanageable: writing-paper, books—even the stiff book covers—everything of the kind curls up and becomes unsightly; boots that fitted with comfort in England shrink to such an extent that they are useless; nothing escapes, not even one's person, lips crack, and nostrils and eyes sting; and altogether one has days of intense personal discomfort. Moreover, the fine almost invisible sand-dust searches into everything, and very soon both my watches were affected; next my camera shutter went wrong, and later on a rifle and gun. These latter were the greatest mishaps to befall me during Harmattan, and they were serious enough at the onset of an expedition.

Thus it will be seen that at Kano there is already something of sand and bleakness, and, to a considerable degree, it is therefore relative to the boundless Sahara to the north, while the advent of the Harmattan and driving sands bring to one the very atmosphere of the great lone wastes of the hinterland. And in keeping with such impressions, and enhancing them, stands the strange, and ancient, and powerful city of Kano, which in its unique earth-built aspect has all the character of a city of the mystical northern desert and little or none of the character one is accustomed to see in Nigeria. Perhaps, most of all, Kano impressed me with its atmosphere of age: the gigantic ramparts around it, and many of the quaint mud dwellings were obviously time-worn, in that inimitable manner of things that are unmistakably ancient, and carry about them for ever the rudiments of the craftsmanship of strange races that have passed and gone for all time.

And though we may know from hearsay that great powers in race and religion have lived within the walls of Kano to fight and struggle for power and existence through ages of History—as is the destiny of kingdoms—it is difficult to realise how slowly time has advanced in this secluded back-eddy, and how very close the past is to the present, until you have walked within the ancient walls and fallen under the spell of the old-world character of the people, and their dwellings, and their customs.

Undoubtedly this atmosphere of the Past which hangs so

closely about Kano remains there because the town so long lay out of the way of the ever-hurrying feet of that advancing, engulfing "civilisation" of our age which is the ruling "God" of the white man in his own land, whereso ever that be, or in any other land that he has fallen heir to through the honourable, or mayhap—be it whispered—dishonourable enterprise of a bygone grandparent.

It was as late as 1902 that the white man came before the gates of Kano, demanding admittance, and since the aggressors were the great "Bature," and had many rifles (a few arms collectively are invariably construed as *many* by timid, untaught natives), the Hausa inhabitants, who were at discord with the Fulani, who were their masters at the time, and deserted by the cowardly Emir Alieu, forthwith bowed before Destiny with true Negro fatalism, and accepted British rule without serious dispute, and without making any kind of stout-hearted defence against the undermanned punitive expedition that was sent out at the time; a fact to their discredit, for they were in their thousands.

It would appear, from records, that the pact between conqueror and vanquished was a friendly one, and of such wisdom that the change of rule was not a drastic one and brought no tyranny; in fact, the hands of the Crown's Trustees were laid so lightly upon the people in directing their administration, that they (the natives) lost none of their ancient characteristics or pride of race at the time of small beginnings of acquaintance with Europeans; so that almost up to the present day Kano remained to all intents and purposes completely native and original, and a great and powerful centre of the Hausa people and of Mohammedanism. It is at the present time that the careless breath of civilisation has swept inevitably—for it is useless to expect to gainsay

Destiny—in from the South, and has cast a blight upon the simplicity of the natives, with unnatural consequences to their frail character.

In 1911 the Nigeria railway was laid down to Kano. In 1914—about six years ago—there was less than a score of Europeans within the British segregation about a mile east of the Hausa City, and at the time of my journey, early in 1920, somewhere about six score; the former a barely perceptible number amongst the vast native population; the latter just enough to have started the swing of the pendulum of commerce and speculation which already promises to change a fine old world that is rare to a new world that will grow commonplace. I treasure old things, as I fancy we all do, and therefore cannot refrain from regret when I see something that is dear totter on the brink of destruction—so often it cannot be saved by reason of circumstances or environment, and it goes out for ever, for the passing of the *Old* is just as inevitable as the coming of the *New* beneath the propelling will of Destiny.

The population of Kano is a fluctuating one, on account of the nomadic propensities of many of the people, and I think I am right in saying that there are on that account no exact statistics concerning numbers. There is said to be an average population of about 80,000 inhabitants in Kano, which dwindles to about 60,000 in the "off season," and rises to about 100,000 in the height of the trading season, when ground-nuts are marketed.

The province of Kano, of which the City of Kano is capital, has a population of 2,871,236,[4] which is a much greater number than that contained within any other province in Nigeria, its nearest competitor having barely half that total.

Those few figures may serve to proportion the extent of

the importance of Kano; but let me lay statistics aside henceforth, for I would fain wander back in random fashion within the old gaunt walls of the city and examine the quaintness and the rudeness wherever dust-lain mysterious lanes may lead me.

Within the walls of Kano the city is composed of thousands of diminutive hutments, which crouch low and are huddled together as if to gain each from the other strength, and companionship, and protection, which is indeed the intention in a land which suffers from the sting of driving, biting sandstorms, and knew in the Past the swoop of attacking enemy.

The huts, and the enclosure walls about them, are built with reddish clay-soil taken from pits in the neighbourhood, and, with the addition of water and plant fibres, kneaded into a plaster which, after it has been applied, sets very hard. Dwellings so built are cool and weather-worthy for the greater part of the year, but at the time of the Rains some damage is usually wrought by the heavy wash of water, and repairs are necessary thereafter.

In appearance the dwellings are stoutly built at the hands of patient, careful labour (for the natives are not a little skilled in their work), and, though they have seldom ornament of any kind, their simple lines and odd and primitive planning have an attraction, and a novelty that is peculiar, apparently, to the walled-towns on the northern borders of negro-land.

Kano, like most native towns, has grown upon no preconceived lines, with the result that it is to-day a happy-go-lucky jumble of dwellings that in many cases appear to just save themselves from complete imprisonment by the number of lanes that provide, by the genius of necessity, a way of escape to the encompassed dwellers. Throughout the whole city runs an amazing network of street-lanes, zigzagging and turning and twisting in every conceivable direction and holding to no true course for any appreciable distance, which is the outcome of the numerous den-builders having built their little dwellings wherever an open space or a corner was available, without preconceived attempt to form the whole in any kind of symmetrical plan.

From the outside the openings in the severe lane walls—which are 8 to 10 ft. high—do not invite a stranger to enter freely into the privacy of these native dwellings, but, not wishing to miss anything, I one day plucked up courage and asked of an aged woman, who was squatted on the ground at a doorway in a lane, if she would show me the interior of her house?

But before making my request I tactfully gave her the long formula of Hausa greeting:

Self:—Sanu sanu! (good day!)

Aged woman:—Sanu kaddai! (thank you!)

Self:—Sanu da aiki! (blessings in your work!)

Aged woman:—Sanu kaddai! (thank you!)

Self:—Enna lafia? (how are you?)

Aged woman:—Lafia lau! (very well!)

Self;—Enna gajia? (how is weariness?)

Aged woman:-Babu gajia! (none!)

Self:-Enna gidda? (how is your house?)

Aged woman:—Lafia lau! (very well!)

Self:—Madilla![5] (thank God!)

Aged woman:—Madilla! (thank God!)

Which formula the Hausa native dearly loves to be greeted with, since it is the habitual form of friendly salutation; and it now brought me good-natured bidding to enter.

Across the door-opening in the wall I stepped from the lane into the yard or compound—a small open space with high walls on all sides— which was clean, though earthen and dusty, and contained a few naked infants that played about the hut doors in company with a pair of young goats of an age to be nursed and nourished at home, while a few bantam-sized African fowls scratched for pickings where wooden mortar stools and pestle poles on the ground told that the industrious women of the house had lately been crushing grain for the forenoon meal. There was not, contrary to the usual custom, any tree or bush preserved within the narrow limits of the yard for sun-shelter.

The yard I had entered contained two huts built of the same clay-soil material as the outside walls, and, bending almost double, I entered the low dark doorless opening which gave admittance to the home of the old woman, and stood then in dim light in a tiny den which had only a few feet of space altogether. Indeed, such dwellings contain area of so little extent that if a long woodframed couch is placed therein, or a grass mat for reclining upon is laid upon the floor, one full side of the room is taken up. No window lit the interior—though there are sometimes one or two narrow loopholes near the ceiling in huts of this type—and but a dim light filtered indoors from the sun-shadow that fell athwart the low doorless opening; the hard-baked floor was of the same red clay-soil as the rest of the dwelling and of the colour of the ground outside; the flat ceiling— which showed the ant-proof dum palm beams and the spans of grass matting between, which carried the weight of earth that composed the roof overhead—was densely hung with cobwebs and black with the wood-smoke from years of night-fires and cook-fires, which had also dimmed the rough red walls. There was no furniture in the hut, nothing that had the purpose of an ornament, for though the Hausa people are excessively fond of ornament on their persons, strangely enough no such taste is reproduced in their dwellings. Upon the floor lay a clean grass mat, whereon the inhabitants are wont to crouch around the food-bowl at meal-time, or individuals recline in sleep in the heat of the height of the day; a few calabash drinking-bowls and bowls for drawing well-water hung from the ceiling and from the wall, where also a well-used bow and a buck-skin sheath of arrows hung from a peg.

From this room a short dark passage led to the other hut, which was of exactly the same character and aspect as the first, except that therein two comely women, in bright cotton garb, had taken refuge in shyness of the white stranger—wives, no doubt, of the proprietor, who was not for the moment at home. A few Hausa words to them in friendliness and a coin to the old woman, and I passed outside into the daylight again and on my way, followed by the grateful "Na gode, na gode! (thank you, thank you!) of the old woman, who was much flattered over the advent of a white man to her humble "gidda" (abode).

Therein I have described one native home in Kano, and in describing one have portrayed the type, for, except in minor details, they are all very similar. They are, in fact, when all is said and done, but the simple primitive shelters of an outdoor people of an old world, who are content for the most part to make shift, somewhat in gipsy fashion, with the rude necessities of life like unto the wild things about them.

Of course there are, in addition to the mass of dwellings, the Mohammedan mosque, and Sultan's Palace, and market-stalls, which have importance and peculiarities of their own and complete the city as a whole; but the great novelty of the place lies along the lanes and about the mud huts of the crowded populace, and upon the rampart walls that stand stalwart guards through the ages.

In the Past it would appear the natives of Kano lived almost altogether within the ramparts of the city, as was the defensive custom of rival centres throughout the territory; for tribal wars were continual in those days, one group fighting another, one city besieging another to such an extent that safety was only to be found behind stout walls and lines of archers, while, in times of disturbance, the bush outside remained a deserted no-man's-land.

Thus to withstand siege Kano had more than its crowded streets of dwellings within the walls that enclosed an area of 7¼ square miles; there was open ground where goats and cattle and camels could be herded and fed for a time when threat of attack should drive them in from the outside; there were ponds and pits of water, even in the dry season, where beasts could be watered, and deep wells to supply the people. So that with their herds of animals to slaughter for meat, and secreted grain stores, and abundant water, the inhabitants were in a strong position to withstand siege in the good old days of high adventure—days not long removed so far as they are concerned.

Within the walls, also, are the twin hills Goron Dutse and Dalla, outstanding though not massive in area, but most notable because they are the only hills in view on any side over the distance of cleared land and bushland of the surrounding country, so that they are like sentinel posts and fortresses to outside eyes.

Lastly, and most striking feature of all in this place of strange reflection of ancient customs, there are the great ramparts which completely surround the city. They are the very embodiment of strength, towering above all else—of great width and height, and one solid mass of welded clay-soil. Indeed, the whole enclosure is so colossal that one cannot but be filled with amazement when endeavouring to conceive an imaginary estimate of the labour and enthusiasm that the masters and their subjects and their slaves must have put into the work. At some time or other one can easily imagine that countless thousands of naked natives swarmed upon those walls, intent on one great purpose, like so many droves of tireless working ants. The walls are 40 ft. wide at the base, and rise, tapering to 4 to 6 ft. width at the top, to a height of 30 ft. and more. The parapet is punctuated with regular openings to accommodate the drawn bows of archers when kneeling on the ledge or pathway which is on the inside of the top of the wall. The great wall which encircles the city is no less than 11 miles around its circumference, while there are thirteen tunnel-like gloomy entrances, through the great width at the base, on main roadways that diverge from the city, so that exit or entrance can be made from any side. In the side walls of the tunnel entrances there are room-like cavities excavated which apparently accommodated the guard in time of war.

The hour to enter Kano by one of these gates is in the cool of the late afternoon, for at that time you will find that the somnolence which the excessive heat of noonday lays upon the easy-going inhabitants has lifted and that there is a great stir of joyous life about the city. The earth streets and lanes are filled with natives bent on one occupation or another, for Kano is at heart a regular hive of industry—"the great emporium of Central Africa," as Dr. Barth described it on his travels in 1850. It is the principal hour in the market-place, and women and men pass thereto with baskets of wares carried with easy grace upon their heads; laden donkeys, dun-coloured or grey, pass market-wards too; and long-gaited camels, and sometimes lean-ribbed, big-boned oxen, all converging into Kano in the one direction, whence issues the hum of many voices telling where a multitude has already gathered.

A STREET-LANE IN KANO.

AN ENTRANCE IN THE MUD WALLS OF KANO.

The market is comprised of long streets of low, roofed-in open stalls, wherein the wares are exposed upon the ground within an allotted space, while the gown-clad Hausa merchants kneel behind them with becoming solemnity and do business. You may see upon some stalls British cotton, and British ironmongery, and British cigarettes which have been imported, and a few other things; but for the most part the wares are native, and you can single out baskets of raw cotton, bobbins of home-spun thread, and stout Kano Cloth—which is renowned in Nigeria—the weaving and dyeing of which is a large industry. Also the sale of hides, and leather-work, and basket-work, and pottery are local industries of importance that bring wares to the market; while tailors and blacksmiths flourish at their trades. There are food-stalls, where such staple foods as millet, and guinea corn, and maize, and beans (whole or ground to flour) are exposed for sale in calabash bowls or grass-woven baskets;

30 *Angus Buchanan*

and tomatoes, onions, yams, sugar-canes, and the pepper and plant-leaves that go to make up the local pottage condiments. The meat market is set apart, which is wise, for it is fly-ridden and odoriferous, and beef and mutton and choice parts of offal (of which natives are particularly fond) are there exposed for sale.

The merchants of the stalls are principally of the Hausa race, and there are a few Arabs. But in the cattle-market, which is also on one side, the natives are often Fulani and Beri-Beri, who have brought in cattle, sheep, goats, and camels from distant bush where their herds roam.

There are some horses for sale in the cattle-market; high-mettled, Arab-like beasts that are often very attractive, but which, very unfortunately, are almost invariably gone at the houghs through the stupid native habit of throwing a galloping horse suddenly back on its hindquarters on hard ground to make a dramatic halt before an audience or a king's house, by means of pressure on the locally-made cruel bit-iron which projects on to the roof of the mouth.

It may be gathered at this stage that the local market of Kano is well equipped to supply the wants of the primitive people. Moreover, the whole interchange of trading is so extensive, that there is a very wholesome buying and selling within its own circle which employs almost everyone and makes the city doubly self-supporting and self-sufficient.

This market within the old city, in its entirety, is the everyday mart of the inhabitants and does not greatly concern the white traders, who buy, at their own warehouses in the European segregation outside the walls, their stacks of hides and tons of ground-nuts and beans, which are the rich exports from the place.

There is also some European trade in cattle and sheep, which are railed for the consumption of people at "down country" stations and on "the Coast."

But it is now time to pass on from the market-place and return to quarters, though the loitering crowd that presses about the stalls is so dense that it is difficult to pass through it, and the din of the eager voices is deafening. However, once clear of the congestion and noise, it is very pleasant walking or riding slowly home under the spell of a closing day. Hundreds of natives are still on the dusty roads, arriving joyfully at the journey's end with burdened animals, from distant parts, or coming from the fields or villages near-by when the work of the day is finished; all gladly and contentedly returning home, or coming to a haven of rest, while the sound of pounding pestle-poles in their mortar stools resounds methodically in the still air to declare to all ears that industrious housewives are preparing the evening meal.

You may hear also, about this time, the monotonous tom-tom of small drums arising from the direction of a group of hutments, and the loud voice of a functionary raised in peculiar declaration to call forth neighbours; from which it may be understood that there is gaiety afoot in some quarter where a wedding-dance is starting. Such sounds on the evening air are very pleasant, as are all sounds close to nature when they are explanatory of familiar living things and joy of life to anyone who is overtaxed with the silence of the lone places, as are many men of the caravans and of the bush who drift into Kano from afar.

Passing through a shadowed gateway, named "Nassarawa," in the eastern wall, you may leave the strange old city behind in the dusk and take the straight road to the white man's town while snow-white flocks of Cattle Egrets fly gracefully and softly across the eve-lit sky to their night grounds, and satiated vultures and kites clamber heavily to their roosting-perches on gnarled old solitary trees to gather on each one in colonies.

CHAPTER III
HAUSA, CURRENCY, CAMELS, TRAVELLING

A T Kano I picked up two more natives to accompany me on my journey, a Hausa youth named Mona and a half-caste named Outa, while the interviews with applicants were not without amusement, since conversation was carried on in my somewhat amateur Hausa, with John privileged to look on, and give his comical but shrewd opinion of the character of his probable fellow-travellers—and he had his strong likes and dislikes, though he judged his subjects solely by eye, for he could not speak Hausa, as is the case with many natives of other tribes, and in particular with coast boys.

Languages are very numerous in Africa, and to know them all would be a great task, but every European on the West Coast knows and makes use of the amusing native *patois* termed "Pigeon English," which is the crude English that natives learn to speak who come much in contact with white men. And when one begins to form sentences in Hausa, and troubles to translate them literally into English, it is amusing what peculiar phrasing is arrived at, and how similar it is to the *patois* of the natives. Thus here are some literal translations of some of the Hausa sentences I used:

Interrogating native hunter.

"You, you make king of hunting in your town?"

"I make journey, I reach Aïr, after so I return within Kano when my work I finish. You agree you come far together with me?"

"Money how much you wish you do work with me moon one one?"

"You agree you do month ten (with me)?"

Consulting a chief for information of local hunting-ground and local hunter.

"I want I may collect birds and animals of bush."

"I want I may flay them and I look inside of them."

"I wizard am. I carry them and I show them to white men wizards in land (of) Europe."

"Not I wish I make journey quick because I want I catch them all."

"I want I may make hunting where grass it makes tall."

"I want I may make hunting where rivers they make many: a place of lake and marsh."

"You are able you give me a hunter, he come along with me: he point out to me a bush good?"

Translation of Hausa speech to natives when camping and hunting.

"We shall alight here."

"Perhaps we sit here days ten and four."

(Or in opposite case): "We shall sit here little little, not we shall delay place this. I will go I make hunting at (this) night.

You it is necessary you sit; you look (my) camp. Do not you sleep."

"I will take (my) gun, I will go, I will make of hunting now."

"You bring trap of iron."

"We will sit here, we will watch in silence."

"Do not you make (of) moving."

"Beast that it is with a bad wound, we will follow it."

The natives secured at Kano completed my personnel for hunting—Sakari and Mona being available for gun-bearing, bag-carrying, and skinning, Outa as horse-boy, and John as cook and caretaker of his master, for he had already attached himself to me with the sincerity of a faithful servant and was now watchful of my welfare, especially taking upon himself to warn me when he detected any "slim" manœuvring over camels or food or gifts by cunning characters that came about camp or were met on our wayfaring.

Delays always seem to dog the start of a prearranged journey—the more anxiously planned, the more sure some fateful hitch at the last moment—and my experience at the "end of the line" in Nigeria was no exception. At Kano the large quantity of stores of food and hunting accessories that were to carry me through barren country for about a year lacked almost all gun and rifle ammunition and an important crate of apparatus for entomological work; all of which had missed the steamer at Liverpool; which advice I received in due course.

However, as the neighbourhood of Kano had been unworked by collectors, it was not unprofitable to make a beginning there, while observations alone would give me a good ground work to go on as I moved further north, for by being familiar with species that inhabited the Kano region of Northern Nigeria, I could the more surely detect types peculiar to localities or given latitudes as I encountered them in the Sudan.

Therefore I did not stay many days in Kano while waiting the arrival of the lost supplies, and with the aid of native carriers moved out with all my baggage to camp about six miles north of the town near to a small village named Farniso.

My experiences there need not be unduly dwelt on. The country-side was for the most part thickly populated and well cultivated, and collecting was not of an exciting order. There were no antelope in the neighbourhood, and jackals and foxes were the largest animals I collected. Jackals were very plentiful, and I have seen their dens even in the walls of Kano.

Reports reached me that there were a few lions in low-lying country on the Hadeija river, where it passes through N'gourou, and also that there was some good big-game country east of Kano towards Maidugari (nearing Lake Chad territory), and I have no doubt but that such reports were true, although I had no opportunity of hunting in those localities. I judge that the big-game hunter who journeyed to Kano would not find his hunting there, but would seek it some days away to the east or the west or the north. I know not the territory any great distance east and west, but I know something of it northwards, and anon will explain where game lies *where I have seen*.

Though collecting in the neighbourhood of Kano was not exciting, bird life was attractive and abundant, as were small mammals, and my days were well filled hunting in the early morning or late afternoon during the hours of feeding and movement of the creatures of the underbush, who dislike as much as humans do the intense heat of an overhead sun, and skinning and setting specimens all through the day, and after dark at night, in camp. During the few weeks I remained camped near Farniso I collected 207 birds and 83 mammals, and also a quantity of butterflies and moths.

In due course the lost ammunition arrived and a great anxiety was lifted from my mind, for new regulations with regard to arms and ammunition being exported from England were so complicated at the time, that long delay, or even loss of authorisation was possible if not probable; and I would have been in a nice predicament and completely crippled without this item, which was so indispensable to me on my journey. I assure you I could have shouted with sheer joy when I saw the small weighty business-like boxes coming into camp on the heads of carriers that were groaning under their loads.

The arrival of ammunition stores left me free to begin the camel journey northward over the boundary into French territory, though I was still short of the crate of entomological apparatus— which did not reach me till more than a month later, forwarded by courtesy of the French officials.

In departing from Kano I would say good-bye to the last post that boasted of civilisation and pass "out of the world," for there are surely few places on the face of the earth more remote and God-forsaken than the interior Sahara of Central Africa—as in due course I was to learn; though in this I was to some extent prepared by study of bare incomplete maps, and in finding how difficult it was to glean any information of the country in England before sailing. But I was not prepared to find how little was known of the country at Kano, where I had calculated I would probably learn much about my journey ahead, whereas, in fact, I gained practically no information from the few white men there, and very little from natives, who were much given to reticence with strangers, or, if free-spoken, to wild exaggerations. I did not meet a single Englishman or Scot in Kano who had been across the boundary into French territory as far as Zinder, which is a ten days' camel journey north, and it is strange but really true that almost as little is known of the Territoire du Niger in Nigeria as in England, though the two former are next-door neighbours. But so far as travelling to Zinder is concerned, apart from Zinder being in French Territory, it can be readily understood why British Europeans do not make the journey from Kano if one can realise the desolation of the country and the exhausting heat of the African sun, which makes such a trip, merely for the sake of sight-seeing, altogether uninviting.

By reason of preparing to enter this land that knew the sadness and solitude of "the lone places" rather than even the rudiments of civilisation and commerce, I had perforce to carry all stores necessary to life; and I must carry money also—not a little, but a quantity sufficient to last me over a protracted period. Therefore, my last act on the eve of departing was to ride into Kano to draw money from the bank. And through the kindness of the manager of the Bank of British West Africa, who rightly viewed my task in the light of one of national importance and not one of trade, I was enabled to have the large quantity I required issued to me in silver; which was a generous concession on his part, and of the utmost value to me, for silver was at that time at a premium, and one could purchase at least 25 per cent. more with coin than with paper-money, which found ill-favour with the natives.

There are two reasons why notes, which, at the time of my visit to West Africa, were causing much inconvenience and concern to traders in Nigeria and to the military officials in the French colony, are disliked. In the first place, many of the natives are unable to read the value printed on paper-money, both the actual figures and the wording being in English, so that when it is tendered in purchase, they are sometimes doubtful of the value they are receiving; whereas with coin they can easily judge the different values by the variety of size. Secondly, it is the habit of the natives to conceal their wealth in a secret hole in the walls of their huts or in the ground, and paper-money is not adapted for such a purpose, since it is not impervious to damp in the rainy season, nor the ravages of white ants or mice at all times. Furthermore, the "brown paper" shilling currency is a poor affair at best, and not durable to the large amount of outdoor handling which money receives at the hands of the natives, and whenever a note becomes torn, it is looked upon as valueless among themselves, and quickly reaches the white man's store, where it is known it will be accepted and taken off their hands.

So, with knowledge of the drawbacks of paper, I gleefully returned to camp with my supply of silver, and that night secreted the major portion of the coin in various ammunition boxes in the hope that it would in that way escape detection and plunder on my long journey. Silver in quantity is very heavy to transport, but that was fully compensated for—for had it not the power to put one on good terms at once in all dealings necessary with natives? Further, I found it unnecessary to make exchange to French coin once I had crossed the Frontier, since the English shilling and two-shilling piece were acceptable everywhere.

I secured ten camels for my journey to Zinder, and not, in a limited time, since it was ground-nut season, when transport animals are in great demand, being able to obtain the full number required to transport my loads, which weighed close on 4,000 lbs., I had to fall back on oxen to complete the complement, taking four of the latter to carry loads equivalent to that which two camels could carry. Camels can load 300 to 400 lbs.

The camels of Hausaland and the Territoire Militaire du Niger are the one-humped race that are named "Rakumi" in Hausa and "Alum" in Tamāshack, and they are the outstanding transport animals of the country. Indeed, without camels it is difficult to see how the inhabitants of the interior Sahara could subsist, for they are, in essentials, the only animals truly adapted to long journeys in barren land, where water and food are often very scarce. The distance they can travel with 300 to 400 lbs. loaded on their backs, and their uncomplaining endurance is altogether marvellous, and it would be a man of poor appreciation indeed who knew their habits and had not praise for them.

Donkeys and oxen are two other animals of transport which are used on routes that are not too severe, and donkeys in their patience and endurance have some of the commendable traits of camels, and are capable of accomplishing long journeys if not too heavily loaded—100 to 150 lbs. is a fair load—though they are slower in getting over the ground. Oxen, on the other hand, are of secondary value as transport animals, and are seldom satisfactory on a journey of any length, for they do not harden well to their work, and often break down tamely under a prolonged burden. This is because the heat of day is very trying on them when *en route*, while it has little effect on either camels or donkeys.

As Aïr, and the section of the Territoire Militaire through which my journey led me is the home of the camel, and since I travelled hundreds of miles with those fine animals, perhaps a few remarks concerning them would not be out of place.

The market-price of camels in 1920 at Kano and Agades was about £8 for a young beast 4 years old, and about £15 for a full-grown animal 9 to 15 years old. Those prices, even though they have risen considerably since the war, like everything else even in such remote parts, must appear small if it is taken into consideration that camels require to be nourished and reared for 8 to 10 years before they have reached maturity and are really fit to join the caravans and bring recompense to the owner. On one occasion I saw a young camel of 4 years, small and still with a semi-calf look about it, being ridden by a Tuareg who was a lightweight; but to break a camel at that age is quite exceptional, if not foolish, for in all probability this early labour, before bones are hardened and muscles full and set, spoils the ultimate development of the animal. Some camels are considered developed enough for short journeys when 6 years old, though they are seldom fully matured until 8, 9, or 10 years, while they reach their prime about the age of 15 years; afterwards they begin to lose a little ground, but are often quite useful and strong up to and over 20 years. At an age of 30 years a camel may be said to be altogether beyond work.

In colour there is considerable range among camels, the most common variety in this territory being light buffish-brown, somewhat resembling sand, while piebald and brindled camels are also numerous, the latter having random patches of white on a surface that is chiefly dull lead-like blackish-grey. Those piebald and brindled beasts are reputed to be an Aïr race, but how far that is true I had no opportunity of proving, though I can vouch for having seen among the Aïr mountains more camel-calves of that colour than any other. Moreover, it is a splendid protective colour against the mountain background of blackish rock and pools of sand, so that the claim has at least that in its favour. A colour that is not very common among camels is pure white, while one that is quite rare is rich tawny reddish buff. I have seen a score of animals of the former colour, but only two of the latter.

A HAUSA NATIVE RIDING AN OX, KANO

CATTLE OF HAUSALAND.

In selecting camels to make up a caravan, it is problematical whether you get good-tempered or bad-tempered beasts, and one should be optimistic enough to accept the bad with the good and put up with the annoyance of saddling and loading cantankerous individuals, for there is no caravan was ever without them. But if you wish to use a camel for hunting—and they are exceedingly good for the purpose, being very noiseless of foot—great care in selection should be exercised, and only a tried animal should be used which is good-tempered and taught that it must not roar as you dismount to commence your stalk on sighting game. The awkward and somewhat wooden appearance of camels does not lead one to associate much intelligence with them, but to think so is a mistake, and if one desires to have a really good hunting camel, I know of no better method to secure it than to select a good-natured beast from the rank and file, and hand-feed it with tit-bits of vegetation, and pet it when mounting and dismounting, and let no one else saddle it or ride it, and before long you will be astonished to find that you have won a queer pet and a useful and obedient comrade. It will have been gathered that it is the noisiness of the brutes that has to be guarded against when hunting, and that is so, for they are fearful beasts to roar on the slightest provocation. Besides being timid animals, they are very tender skinned, and almost all of them emit a loud complaining roar whenever they are touched by a human hand or there is the slightest movement in the position of the saddle in mounting or dismounting; while if an animal happens to be suffering with horrible septic saddle-sores, such as are very common, it is sure to make a terrifying uproar whenever approached.

When travelling with a caravan, it is usual to commence to load up before daylight and get well started on the way before sunrise, which is about 6.30 a.m., or—especially if there be a moon—to make a start at 2 or 3 a.m. in the night, and travel the greater part of the day's journey free from the rays of the exhausting sun. On such occasions the camels are gathered in at sundown on the eve before from browsing among the acacias, and made to lie down by the camp-fire, so that they are at hand when the camel-men go to work in the darkness. Then, when the hour to start comes round, logs that have been collected the night before are kindled to make a blazing fire, and by the light of the flames the loads are securely roped and loaded across the pack-saddles, so that equally balanced packs rest on either side, while throughout the process the black bush silence of the night is rudely broken by the deep querulous roars of the camels in protest against being handled. Loading up in the poor light of night is a slow process, and in my case three or four men usually took from an hour to an hour and a half to load ten to fifteen camels. But the secret of a smooth journey is to begin the day with loads thoroughly secure and well balanced so that they will not annoy the bearer; and with bulky loads, such as the chop-boxes and collecting-cases of the white man, which are unfamiliar and clumsy both to the natives and their beasts, it requires considerable care in loading to be reasonably sure of a well-ordered start. When things do not go well, it is a mistake for the traveller to become impatient and abuse or hurry the camel-men in the early morning, when tempers are apt to be short, for although they are undoubtedly slow in their methods, they know their work and their animals, and will make the better loads if left alone, and you merely lend a hand here and there, and joke with them over their work, and thus gain their good-will and confidence. As to the type of saddle, a serviceable and simple saddle is made of wood in this fashion: first there are two arch-shaped pieces which are made to fit over the back of the animal, and which rest before and behind the hump, while underneath them are bound leather pads filled with palm fibre, so that the saddle is comfortably received on the camel's back; secondly, from the back and front pieces there are run four horizontal bars, which are bound in position to the arches with goat-skin or sheep-skin thongs, whereby the saddle is made rigid and complete. It is a very simple piece of construction, but serves the purpose.

Sometimes no saddle is used when carrying good loads, such as bales of grain or salt, which naturally lie very close and compactly to the body of an animal, in which event two long goat-skins are used, puffed out like pillows with filling, which are thrown over the back on either side of the hump, and receive the burdened load ropes which carry the bales in position on the sides.

When loading camels on the first day at the commencement of a journey, or after having been idle for a week or two turned loose in the bush, they are afraid of their unfamiliar loads, and behave like bolting horses or wild colts, and saddles and packs are no sooner secured, and the brutes on to their feet, than they show their ill-humour and everything is thrown to the ground again. Once, twice, even thrice this may happen with three or four camels in the caravan, while it seems as if you will never be able to get out and away on the road. But in the end all are ready and in line and a start is made. But on that day you are sure of trouble *en route* with the fractious animals, and not until the morrow need you expect anything like reasonable order, when you will almost surely find that even the worst of the brutes has become docile and resigned to steady work.

I did not miss any of my share of this sort of experience when the day came for me to set out from Kano—I don't think anyone does. Camels and their Tuareg drivers were in my camp at Farniso ready to start on the morrow (12th January). That evening trouble began: the camel-men, not having finished their private bargaining in Kano and seeking an excuse to delay, had put their heads together, with the result that they concocted a story that they had not enough rope to cope with the tying of the awkward loads of the white man—which was true, in fact, though anyone might know that it was not necessary to go to Kano to secure them with a village close at hand. However, knowing their homes were distant, and that it might be long before they had again occasion to visit Kano, I gave permission for one of them to go back, provided he would start there that night when the moon rose at 11.30 p.m., which he promised to do. Being easy-going and trusting at that time, which was before I had much knowledge of the plausible and sly-tongued Tuareg, I turned in and slept soundly—*and so did the cameleer*, for next morning I learned that he had not started for Kano until daylight. This meant that the whole morning was lost—not very pleasant when tents are down and everything you possess is bundled up and roped in camel-loads, and there is nothing left to do but sit on them and smoke innumerable cigarettes and inwardly curse your camel-men and your luck.

The camels were, in the meantime, turned at large to feed in the neighbourhood with their fore-feet hobbled, which was as it should be; and all was right until the man returned from Kano with more ropes *and his purchases of cloth*, and a cameleer hastened out to bring in the animals, but returned in about an hour to say that he could not find two of the camels.

At this stage everything seemed fated to go wrong on this day.

But there is a rift in the clouds even on the worst of days, and in the end the lost camels appeared in view, coming in at a breakneck pace before a mounted camel-man who had skilfully tracked them down in the sand for a long distance and rounded them up. The brutes, though their fore-feet were hobbled, had tried to return to their old haunts in Kano.

It was after 3 p.m. before we got loaded and away on this ill-fated day.

I had arranged before starting that we would camp at Fogalawa, 18 miles away, and it was well I did so, for, after starting out together on the road, I did not see the main part of the caravan again until midnight, since I remained throughout the journey with the tail-end of the line, where an obstreperous and unruly old female camel made the devil's own trouble, and threw her load again and again with most vicious determination. The climax came close on sunset, when the camel-man and I were overheated and dust-grimed and angry over our exertions, and the cantankerous brute cut loose once again, and threw and shattered the chop-boxes and strewed the contents on the road. While bemoaning my ill-luck, and letting tongue run loose on the virtues (?) of our beast of burden, and at a loss to know what to do next, a native chanced to come up with some unloaded camels, and I was able to strike a bargain for a beast to take the place of the unruly one.

Thereafter the journey was a smooth one, but, nevertheless, I had lost so much time on the way that it was midnight before I came into camp behind the last camel, and had been nine hours on a journey that should ordinarily take five and a half to six and a half hours.

So much for the discrepancies of the "first day"; and now

I must return to our starting-point, so that I may tell of the wayside. During the afternoon and through the night in the darkness we travelled over a broad roadway of loose shifting sand that held north through fairly open country that was, in general, under cultivation. Trees were plentiful, growing for the most part singly and not in close-set mass, but they do not impress one with height or stature at this season, though in the Rains the full-leaved trees of any size are imposing and conspicuous enough in most of the flat country between Kano and Kanya. No doubt the whole country has been covered with acacia bush at one time, with an odd large tree shooting above the dwarf forests here and there, and though the acacia bush has been cleared away to give place to cultivation, the big trees have been left standing, since to the toilers in the fields they are harbours of shade from the merciless sun.

Along the road a constant incoming string of caravans of camels and donkeys and oxen passed us, carrying bulging bales of ground-nuts to Kano, for the ground-nut season had begun, and unprecedented prices were being paid for them by the white man, which had created a widespread boom in the district and a tremendous wave of speculative excitement. It was a great year— 1920—of prosperity for the natives of Kano, this last fling of commercial extravagance at the end of the war—a rich year that, in the end, must have left its mark, for one could easily forecast the time to come, when there would be acute comparisons between the heyday of the boom and that other day when the boom must burst, and hearts be sore—for it is hard even for a native to come back to the solid old ground-level after he thinks he has reached a golden citadel in the clouds.

Next morning we continued on our way without any

repetition of trouble with the animals, and the old camel, that had stubbornly refused to carry the white man's boxes yesterday, to-day carried with ease a greater load of ammunition packed in native grass-woven bales. The brute had been nothing more than wildly scared of the strange articles that it had been set to carry.

The road continued broad to-day, but grew ever heavier underfoot with loose sand. By the wayside there was not so much cultivation as yesterday, and few habitations, except at Kore and Minna. We camped in mid-afternoon at the small village of Kanya after a pleasantly smooth journey. It was gratifying, after our trials of yesterday, to see how nicely the camels of a well-ordered caravan move forward over the ground with their soft-footed methodical gait; they get over the heavy sand road not only with their long pacing stride, in which both legs on the same side are lifted together, but also they move with a strange stealthy silence, which is due to the rubber-like give of their soft elastic pads. A further odd and striking detail about the feet of a camel is that, unlike other animals, the fore-feet are larger than the hind-feet.

Travelling by the wayside in inhabited country, if you happen to be near human dwellings, cockcrows will herald in the African dawn from some village hut-top obscure among the bush foliage, and on the third day we were busy with the load-ropes in the chill of late darkness ere the first glad cock-call told of approaching day. Already we had learned that it was wise to travel in the cool hours as far as possible and save our animals from the great heat of day, so long as short nights and loss of sleep were not over-fatiguing to ourselves, or, rather, perhaps I should say to myself alone, for natives have the knack of sleeping in daylight just as easily as in darkness, and throw themselves down in any little patch of tree-shade at the end of a journey and retrieve their night-sleep almost before it is lost: while that I could never do, even if I had not work to attend to.

But there was one native with me who worked long hours without sleep much as I did, and he was the faithful John. On his broad shoulders rested all the petty duties of attending to his master's welfare in camp: a host of small duties indeed, such as cooking meals at any hour— early or late, at noon or midnight; pitching or striking my camp-bed (for I slept in the open); or doing the services of a valet in looking after all my personal belongings, and my toilet, even washing clothes when he had the time to spare—in general, cookboy and houseboy all in one, and a treasure. Moreover, he afforded amusement all round through the medium of his perpetual cheerfulness and expansive grin. Often I have laughed to see him, after the rush of getting ready to start, when he had got the last bundle turned over to the camel-men and his master's camp clear, come saucily forward in his cloth cap and with his cane walking-stick—both relics of the coast which were inseparable from his person— and with a perceptible swagger over his "English" (?) and his importance as the master's boy, grin broadly and ejaculate to the head camel-man: "Come on, come on, Aboki (friend), we wait for you!" which assurance always provoked laughter among the men, while Sakari explained to them in Hausa John's "English" (?), and added to it in the telling.

The Harmattan winds had been very pronounced since starting, and the third day was as bad as its predecessors. So full of sand-dust was the air, that a white cloud hung over the land through which the sun was unable to break clearly. The mane of my horse was white with dust, and, looking on the acacia trees a little way off in the bush, they had the appearance they would bear on a frosty morning, with the fine dust, like white mist, hanging low and falling upon them to lie whitely upon the leaves and boughs.

I noticed at Kanya, and beyond, that the peculiar reddish sand and soil of Kano had given place to ordinary whitish-grey.

On this day we travelled to Jigawa, 18 miles away, on the banks of the Tomas river, which, though it was nothing more than dry bed at this season, is a very considerable stream during the Rains, quite one hundred yards across the floodwater. The place is a small town, with the remains of a stockade about its outskirts, and it contained wells of water and the usual village produce of eggs, fowls, and millet-meal, as well as goats and cattle. It may be stated here that there is no scarcity of water or food experienced anywhere on the journey from Kano to Zinder.

I heard at this village the first news of big game that I had had, and in the cool of the afternoon I went out westward to investigate, and the result of a prolonged hunt through fairly open thorn bush was that I sighted, and viewed through field-glasses, four Red-fronted Gazelle, which the local natives with me said were in fair numbers in the neighbourhood. The beasts, at which I fired one ineffectual shot, were very wild, and gave me the impression that they were disturbed often by the natives who hunt them.

The fourth day was a pleasant one, for it entailed only a short ten-mile journey; and I can assure you that a short day after two or three long, hot, and exhausting ones is a very agreeable change.

We camped at noon at Barbara, our day's task finished; and the camels were hobbled and turned out into the scrub bush to enjoy a lengthy repast. Barbara is a large town that lies five miles on the British side of the frontier, and here it was that I bid good-bye to Nigeria for a time. Hence I made it a stopping-place, and an easy day. (I did the same thing many months later, on my return, and was royally received by the Saraki (native king) and his people-a large number of whom were Fulani— who *en masse* spent the day in holiday and dance because the White Man had safely returned and was glad.)

On the morrow we crossed the boundary and entered French territory, having crossed the line about an hour after starting where it lay between the two small villages of Baban Mutum (British) and Dashi (French); places, like many others, that were not shown on either of the incomplete maps I possessed, which were the best I could procure in England.

In the afternoon we halted and camped at Magaria, where there is a small French fort commanded by a European officer, with native troops under him. Here I was most cordially welcomed to French soil, and enjoyed the frank, unfettered hospitality that for ever is to be found with the big-hearted men of the Lone Places. Though I was not yet more than eighty-five miles from Kano, a European visitor was rare to the board of this solitary soldier, and so I was made doubly welcome over our cups of good comradeship, though neither could glibly speak the other's tongue, and conversation was carried on for the most part in halting words of Hausa. He was a jovial good fellow, beside being the kindest of hosts, and ere the day was out I think we put the sober mud walls of his little cabin to shame with our gladness and laughter. That he was a lone man could be gleaned from his surroundings and his tastes. For companions about his abode he had a cage full of little waxbills, a grey parrot, two pie-dogs, two cats, and four Dorcas Gazelles— all bird and beast of the country-side, except the two cats, which were Persian. The barrack square and the garden of the Fort afforded him further pleasures in homely hobbies: in the square, young trees had been lately planted to form an entrance avenue and give shade, and to watch them take root and thrive was this man's way with his treasures. And in the garden among the shrubs and vegetables his interest was the same to coax plants that were not indigenous to grow in the sandy, thirsty soil; and that he had some success I can vouch for, for there were beds of such vegetables as carrots, radish, beetroot, peas, and cabbage growing quite fairly at the time of my visit.

As I progressed later on, I found such humble gardens wherever white men were stationed: only a few places in all, it is true, but always a garden to furnish the need for vegetables, which is a pressing one to the health of Europeans in such a barren land as this, for rarely vegetables and no fruit can be obtained from natives. Apropos to this, entering a country of tropical heat, I was not prepared to find that it was devoid of fruit (excepting a limited amount of dates in the rainy season), and the discovery disappointed and dismayed me, I must confess, for it left me on short commons in that respect throughout the expedition. And when one lives for a prolonged period on the unchanging diet of animals that fall to your hunting, the hunger for fruit or vegetable grows ever greater, and is, at times, very difficult to allay.

The sixth day found us on the road at dawn, with Nigeria behind and the caravan well started on the way to Bande, our next halt. On this day and the next, over a belt of about twenty-five miles, country of marked change was passed through, and one got the impression that it was now turning more to desert. Dum palms, in small groups or solitary, sceptral with their tall graceful stems and tufted rustling tops, were now in the landscape, while there was a new sense of open space about one, such as is felt on sea or prairie, which was brought about by the wide views of grass-grown land before one where eye could range for long distances.

With the regularity of routine we were marching off the distance on the map, and each day we camped a stage further on—and a day nearer to Zinder. On the seventh day we made the journey from Bande to Makochia, over a very heavy road of loose sand; on the eighth we camped at Dogo— ever the cruel sand-drifting winds of Harmattan in our faces, while ever we held steadily on, for after camels are loaded at the dawning of day, never halt is made by the roadside until the journey's end is reached and the patient brutes lie down and are relieved of their burdens.

The day of our journey to Dogo was one of particularly fierce storm, and we went forward against a very heavy wind and enveloped in continuous clouds of drifting sand: and, besides, it was so cold that I had to keep on my woollen sweater and khaki tunic throughout the day, although hitherto I had not on any day worn a tunic, and as a rule discarded my sweater an hour or two after the chill of dawn. At Dogo I was forcibly reminded of a snowstorm on the Canadian plains; before the village there is a wide white level stretch of sand almost plant-bare, over which winds and driftings rushed fiercely from afar to pounce madly upon whatever lay across their path. Not snowstorm nor piercing cold are elements of this land, but imagine the soft sand underfoot, like snow, the drifting sand, the snow blizzard, and the sting of the storm in eyes and nostrils and throat as unpleasant as the tang of biting cold, and you have the comparisons that have a very decided resemblance.

The road to Dogo lay over undulating country, pale with dry grass and sand, with a touch of faded green where there were trees in the open spaces. It should be a fair country to look upon in the Rains, but it is for the present inert, and discoloured with the drifting sand, and is a melancholy land indeed.

The country by the wayside had for a time a pronounced fall away to a deep valley visible to the west.

The altitude of Dogo is 1,375 ft., so that we had descended some 300 ft. since leaving Kano.

Dogo is the Hausa for *tall*, but I could gather no particular reason for the name. Had it been called Gara (the white ant), however, I would have well understood, for I have seldom seen an equal to the plague of termites that was here: boots, leggings, articles hung to the wall, every box among the camel-loads, was attacked by the infernal pests as soon as ever we camped and before we had time to prepare rough timber platforms to raise everything off the ground. White ants have to be guarded against everywhere in the Sudan, but I never saw them worse than at Dogo.

Next day, which was the ninth day of our journey, we reached Baban Tubki, six miles south of Zinder, where there were a few small date groves and plentiful well-water, and more luxuriant vegetation than usual. So that I decided that here I would pitch a collecting camp, and with that purpose in view swung the caravan west of the road, and sought a camping-place among the scattered trees and tall grass about a mile away. Camels were unloaded and the packs freed from their many ropings, and the preparations of camp erection were begun—and trekking for the present was at an end. . . .

In the part of the territory of Damagarim through which I had travelled since crossing the frontier there was no great change from that of Nigeria. It was certainly less populated, but the Hausa, Fulani, and Beri-Beri tribesmen were the same, as also was the construction of their grass huts and villages, though some of the latter were somewhat dilapidated and had the aspect of belonging to a poorer or more careless class of natives.

So far as I could tell by daily short excursions into the bush off the road, none of the country I had passed through was notable for big-game; but if I was to hunt in that particular territory, I would start at Jigawa (fifty-six miles north from Kano), and work north as far as Makochia, about fifty miles further on. I know there are Red-fronted and Dorcas Gazelles in that belt, but that is as far as my limited knowledge goes for the present.

By the wayside, each day, I had made notes of every living thing I had seen—bird or beast or butterfly. Now it was my task to set to work and preserve a representative collection of the fauna of Damagarim, and forge one link in the chain of the zoological geography of the country, of which up to the present nothing was known.

CHAPTER IV
A DAY'S WORK COLLECTING

COLLECTING was my constant occupation during the month that I camped and hunted near Zinder.

Now, collecting Fauna for the scientific purposes of large Natural History Museums is work somewhat out of the ordinary; so much so, in fact, that I would like to show clearly what such pursuits entail, and to do this will endeavour to describe some of the actual work in the field.

To begin with, the climate is African: which means, in this territory, that for at least nine months in the year the land knows not rain, and lies like an overdone pie-crust, withering beneath a heat that is too great. Day after day, with unchecked regularity, from the break of dawn, a fierce sun rises rapidly high up in the sky, and as it gains in strength, so a silence settles upon the earth, for so great is its oppression, that at the height of its power it subdues all living things. About 10 a.m. you may notice that the glad sounds of morning have faded—birds are retiring to leafy shades, the boisterous noise of natives at work in the village has died down; before noon the land is wrapped in silent solitude, and Old Sol alone is left in the field.

Hence the time to go hunting in this land is early in the morning or late in the afternoon, when the creatures of the underworld have left their hiding-places and are up and about in eager quest of feeding. For the hunter and his native boys it is also the favoured hour, for, as in travelling, the cool of the day allows of the maximum of exertion without any forfeit of sheer exhaustion which the noonday sun inexorably imposes.

Let us follow the proceedings of a morning's hunting. I have turned wakeful toward dawn, and lie warmly in my blankets awaiting the sound of cock-crowing to tell me the time, for I am without a watch since the sand has damaged both I possess. When I hear the call I listen for, I know full well I must bestir myself if I would go away to the fields in good time. Blankets and bed are provokingly comfortable at that moment, but it is fatal to hesitate, so I call "John!" and at once he answers, for he too has been sleeping lightly; and while I am dressing he lights a camp-fire and prepares tea. Sakari and Mona are also awakened, and sit, with their coloured blankets over their shoulders and drawn about them, huddled before the few embers of a fire that they have rekindled, for there is a chill in the air and they are still half asleep and without vigorous circulation.

When I am ready, we prepare to start. My search is for birds this morning, so I take ·410 shot-gun for collecting small specimens, 12-bore shot-gun for anything larger, and a ·22 Winchester rifle in case I find some wary bird that I cannot get within gun-shot of, and yet may see it watchfully perched within the range of the little rifle. I fill my pockets with cartridges: those for the ·410 loaded with dust for sparrow-sized birds, and with No. 8 for birds of the size of doves; while I carry only No. 6 in the cartridges for the 12-bore gun, which I have found will kill vulture or eagle or bustard—in fact, any bird less than an ostrich. Also, I take an open basket, so that I may carry the specimens I capture with great care and without damage to the plumage, some cotton wool to stop bleeding and fill wounds, and a notebook in which to record the colours of the soft parts before they fade at death—viz. the colour of the eyes, the bill, and the feet.

John stays behind to prepare breakfast and make camp clean and tidy for the day; Sakari and Mona come with me.

I know where I will go—I keep more westerly than yesterday. We go carefully at first over the uneven ground, for it is not yet light, though there is now a faint brightness in the eastern sky. We are well away from camp, and cannot see it when daylight is upon us. I am alert now that the sky has cleared; eyes roam everywhere, catching movement in the undergrowth, among the leaves of big trees, or in the sky. Many birds I see: little brown ones like the undergrowth or ground; pale ones like the sand; dark ones like the trees; or gorgeous ones that have no shy colouring, but are gems unto themselves, that peep out brightly revealed in the dark background of their leafy haunts. I know them all, they are very familiar—for am I not among them every day? I am not concerned with these: I pass on ever observant, ever expectant, knowing that there are others that I will find. . . . Soon I am arrested: I have heard a note that I do not know—so often I am guided in that way. I go forward watchfully in the direction of the sound. . . . I have now marked down the clump of bushes whence the call proceeds. . . . I am within range of it— when I see a long-tailed bird dive from it and disappear in an instant. I have seen that it is a Coly, but not of a race I know. . . . Pray do not think I have lost this valuable quarry, though it has flown and is out of sight. Ah, no! birds that inhabit a favoured thicket are unlikely to fly very far, especially in the feeding hours of morning. So I pause and listen attentively, and anon I think I hear the tell-tale somewhat mournful single-pipe call of the bird I seek, but it is so faint that I wonder if fancy is deluding me. There is no time now to be lost. I hasten forward among the thorn trees that in a belt grow numerously, and the pulse quickens as I again hear the call for certain, and from more than one bird. . . . I feel my way toward the sounds. . . . I am not sure of the direction at first, but as I draw near there is no doubt. The birds are ferreting for leaf-buds among the thick tangle in the centre of a thorn tree (acacia). I get up in time to see them dart away, and succeed in shooting one specimen. But that is not enough, for the species, a long-tailed Coly, with a blue band on the back of the head (*Colins macrourus*), is new to my collection; I must follow them up. So I hunt on for an hour or so, with the result that I capture four; and it has been an exciting chase, for the birds were peculiarly wild, though they are of a kind that are often easy of approach.

I am very warm, and stand beside a tree to smoke a soothing cigarette. I have seen a number of hawks in the air during the morning; now that I am idling in the shade I see another. It is of a species that I have observed before, but that I have never been able to approach—a very large hawk, of even dark leaden-grey colour, with mighty wings and a crested head. The bird swings slowly over the land about a quarter of a mile away, and I give up following it, and drop my eyes to look about nearer at hand.

I had forgotten the incident, when Sakari aroused me with: "White man, dem shafo (hawk) live for tree—look him!" and he pointed away to a small group of tallish trees on our right. Sure enough, following Sakari's directions, I could make out the outline of a heavy bird perched near the top of one of the trees, whence it overlooked the whole countryside. The native had watched it fly and settle there.

Now began a stalk as exciting as one could wish for. I

always look on birds of prey, the hawks and the eagles, as royal game, and feel about the same intense interest in hunting a wild species of them as I do when stalking a particularly fine head of big-game. Between me and my prey there was hardly any tree cover. I could only trust to using the "lie" of the hollows to reach the bird unobserved or at least unsuspected. I ordered the two natives to remain where they were, while I took my shot-gun and started on a wide detour, so that I might reach a little dry streamlet hollow that led in toward the trees. Rapidly, but carefully, after I had got round into position, I advanced, crouching and creeping, toward the bird; and always when I dared to glance ahead I saw my coveted quarry perched in place and unalarmed. When I drew closer I could distinguish the eyes and hooked beak, and saw that the bird was watchful, for it turned its head in one direction and then in another as it looked out over the landscape. . . . Now I was crawling flatwise, bare bruised knees and all, and before long stood breathless among the trees—the bird somewhere overhead. As I moved to get a better view through the branches, the bird swooped from its perch to make off; and then crumpled up in mid-air as the report of my gun rang out. Seldom have I been more satisfied with the sound of the fall of a heavy bird; for many a like stalk have I made after equally rare prize, only to find the sharp-eyed quarry depart when I was half-way on my journey, or sometimes when almost within shooting range.

The natives soon joined me, and having now enough specimens for the work of the day, we turned back to camp.

On the way home I had two fox-traps to visit and lift, for it is not safe to leave them set during daylight, lest browsing goat or village cur stumble into them. The luck of the morning continued, for in the second trap there was a struggling captive—a beautiful buff sand-coloured little fox known as *Vulpes pallida edwardsi*.

This capture afforded the two natives great satisfaction, and, as is their habit, they showed fiendish glee over the downfall of this creature of renowned wit and cunning. If they were not restrained by my presence, I know they would poke it with sticks and jeer at it, and in many ways act with unconscious cruelty, for they have not an atom of pity for such things—no African has. If they were free to kill the fox, they would secure the teeth and the eyes and the skin to secrete the parts about their persons as charms in the firm belief that they thus invest themselves with the high gifts of the animal against the cunning of their opponents or enemies.

Thus finished a morning's hunting. Sometimes, on other days, I would meet with greater success, sometimes with less; and sometimes, too, I would have my days of disappointment, when a rarity was seen and lost through a missed shot or in losing all traces of it in its flight. But the hunter does not readily forget, and naturally memorises a place where he has once found quarry, so that again and again he will revisit it, and often picks up on a later day that which has escaped him at the start.

There were few big-game in the district, and, in my case, for the present, it was not my concern to hunt them, except that I might have fresh meat.

But in addition to ornithological research, I was interested in collecting all kinds of small mammals, and as few indeed were ever seen in daylight, I had to resort almost altogether to steel traps to make my captures, and had mouse-traps, rat-traps, rabbit-traps, and fox-traps set at nights wherever I found an inhabited burrow or den or a frequented "run."

Furthermore I had yet other matters to give thought to, for I was to bring home collections of Lepidopteræ, which entailed long excursions in the heat of the day in quest of butterflies, and patience-trying hours of watching by a lamp-lure in the darkness of night in quest of moths.

Altogether, I can assure you I had no time to weary for companionship or to realise my loneliness, and that was a comforting consideration.

I have described the manner of hunting specimens, and would now turn to the work of preserving them.

I have built a rough-framed grass hut for workshop, close to my tent. When I return in the morning, it is here that the specimens are taken, and work is begun at once, for the temperature is so great that a lifeless carcass cannot be relied on to keep fresh longer than five hours, and will certainly be beyond handling if left to the end of the day. I usually preserve from five to ten specimens in a day, the number depending on size or the success of hunting; while on special occasions I have finished as many as fifteen in a day.

Sakari and Mona, the boys selected at Lagos and Kano to help in skinning specimens, can now be trusted with certain work. The fox had been put out of pain, and, laying it on its back, I make the opening cut in it and start Sakari on the task of skinning. As he proceeds to work the skin off, from the belly upwards, the limbs are drawn inside and severed at the heel of the paws, the tail is pulled out by the root, and in time the skin is clear of the body and drawn off over the neck and head. The limbs are then labelled: "right fore," "left fore," "right hind," and "left hind," and are severed from the carcass at the hip and shoulder joints, and, along with the skull, are scraped clean of flesh and numbered and laid aside to go with the finished skin of the specimen. All the scraps of flesh and fatty matter are then removed from the skin, and I take it over from Sakari to apply a thorough coating of arsenical soap preservative, when it is labelled and completed, and laid aside to dry. It has taken Sakari about an hour and a half to do the work, and when he is finished I set him to partly skin the smaller birds, for he is light-fingered and has considerable skill.

Mona, meantime, is set to work on the large hawk, which proved to be the Banded Gymnogene (*Gymnogenys typica*). A smaller bird may have the wings severed at the shoulder of the carcass as the skinning progresses and the bones drawn inside to be cleaned of flesh and returned into position, but with a very large bird such procedure is impossible, and the wings must be dealt with separately. So I stretch one of the great wings to full expansion, and on the underside make a cut along the full length of it. Mona then proceeds to part the skin from flesh and bone, so that when the skin is fully released above and below the limb, he can remove all flesh. When one wing is complete, and the bones white and clean, he proceeds with the other. Now the main body may be dealt with, and a cut is made from the top of the breast-bone to the tail, and the work of skinning continues, always using maize-meal as well as scalpel in removing the skin, for the former is invaluable for absorbing all moisture, such as saliva, blood, and grease, as the skin is parted from the flesh, and safeguards all danger of soiling the plumage. From the inside the legs are severed from the body at the top of the thigh, and the tail at the base of the big quills, and Mona proceeds with removing the skin from the body—for later the legs may be returned to, the skin peeled down as far as it will go, and the flesh cleaned from the bones. Soon he reaches the shoulders, and breaks off the wing-bones close to the body, and works the skin, which is now freed from the body carcass, slowly up the neck and over the skull; the neck is then cut off at the base of the skull and the carcass thrown away. The skull is carefully cleaned and remains in the skin attached to the bill. When the limbs and skin are all thoroughly cleaned, Mona's work is finished, for so far can I trust him to go, but no further. He has taken fully two hours over the work, and he has nothing else to do for the time being, since he is not yet sufficiently skilled to skin the smaller things. I now take the hawk skin from Mona and thoroughly anoint the skull and neck with preservative soap, fill the eye-sockets with globular balls of cotton wool, to take the place of the live eye, and pass the head back through the neck into its normal position; I then soap all the remainder of the skin, and place a thin layer of cotton-wool over the damp surface as I go along to keep the feathers from becoming soiled should they turn over skinwards as they often do. When that is done, the bird is completely preserved; but still it has to be reformed, so that it will dry in a perfectly natural outstretched posture. With this intention I first take needle and strong thread, and where I see the base of the scapular feathers showing on the inside of the skin, on either side, I pass the thread through each, and tie it so that in doing so the shoulders are brought together—a trick that greatly assists in bringing the wing butts back into their normal place. Next I cut a stout straight stick or rod of the length of the bird, and point both ends. Upon the upper length of this I wrap sufficient wool to fill the neck, and when that is done, it is carefully inserted in the neckskin and the point of the stick forced up into the base of the bill, while the other end is fixed into the root of the tail. The bird-skin is now lying, back-downwards, with a straight firm rod running down the centre of it; round this rod I commence to build the woollen filling, until a form is shaped of the size of the carcass. I then see that the base of the wing-bones and leg-bones are nicely set close into the body, and, that done, draw the skin over the breast into its original position, and hold it in place with a few stitches; and the bird is ready to pick up and have the feathers rearranged with such care that no one may suspect that it has ever been tampered with—work that requires a distressing amount of patience if you desire a beautiful specimen. When every feather is in place, the specimen is laid in a coffin-shaped mould[6] of correct width to hold the wings in place close to the body, and it is then set aside to dry. When quite dry, the specimen is perfectly rigid, and requires no further support, and may be handled freely.

Small birds are treated in the same way, except that there is no difficulty with the wings, but the work is much more dainty, and requires light fingers and a great store of patience.

Some birds, such as ducks and night-jars, cannot be skinned by bringing the neck over the head, as the latter is too large; in such cases an incision is made in the back of the head and the skull worked out through it.

Meantime, while the natives have been employed with fox and hawk, I have worked on the small birds (the Colies), so that by mid-afternoon all are finished and laid aside to dry, with sufficient camphor sprinkled over them to keep ants from attacking the soft parts of the head. I am then free to set out on another search for specimens or to employ my time in setting traps. If I collect in the cool of the evening, I keep specimens overnight, which can be done without fear of decay, and start skinning them at daybreak on the following morning.

My description will, I trust, illustrate something of the

process employed with specimens collected and preserved in the field. You may already know them if you have been "behind the scenes" in an important museum, and have seen the wealth of research specimens that are there, carefully stored away from the strong rays of daylight so that their colour shall not fade. Drawer upon drawer of different species, all uniform in shape and labelled for the purpose: the Type specimens from the locality where the species was first discovered, and specimens from any other part of the world where it has since been found to exist; many rare and immensely valuable; many the absolute proof of vastly important records that have gone to establish the Natural History of the world, and valuable as the parchments of the historian or the relics of the antiquarian. There you may actually see how the collector makes up his skins in the field, and why they are made, and how the peoples of the world come to know all the creatures that inhabit it.

CHAPTER V
ZINDER

Z INDER is a very strange town: strange because of its great size in so isolated a position; strange because of the nature of its site and old-world obsolete composition.

Kano, though it is the commercial metropolis of the Western Sudan, is first and foremost the capital of the province of the same name by reason of its large population and importance; and in like manner so we find Zinder, the capital of Damagarim, vastly larger than any fellow-village in the territory—a unique and imposing place, lost in a wilderness of great spaces and little peoples.

It is difficult to give those "back home" a fair conception of the solitude of Zinder. But let us suppose for the moment that England and Scotland are wilderness—without "made" roads, without mason-built houses or cottages—and all England covered with scrub-wood of a great sameness, wherein, concealed among the foliage, a few natives have settlements of primeval gipsy kind, while Scotland, we picture, in fancy, as a mountain-land of barren rock, with lowlands of desert sand, and almost no inhabitants at all.

Zinder is 140 miles from Kano, and Agades, at the southern foot of the Aïr mountains—and the only other old-world town on my route—is 257 miles north of Zinder. Suppose we take London to represent Kano, and set out to walk with a caravan of loaded camels toward the north of England. Days pass, and we see a few gipsy-constructed villages by the wayside—nothing more; but when we approach Sheffield, we are surprised to see a large fortified town appear before us, in the distance, standing in the great wilderness alone. This we can take to represent Zinder, for from London to Sheffield is about equidistant as from Kano to Zinder. If you would continue the journey as far as Edinburgh or Glasgow, you should imagine that you have passed from the scrub-wooded land into desert, and that either of those Scottish towns may represent Agades, for from Sheffield to Edinburgh is about equidistant as from Zinder to Agades. Therefore, to realise the solitude of Zinder, you require to imagine that Sheffield stands alone in her dignity in all the land between London and Edinburgh; and if you would picture even greater solitude, such as invests isolated Agades, you may imagine Edinburgh as a straggling town, not large, but steeped in ancient history, and that it is the only town in the length and breadth of Scotland, the earth's surface of which we have imagined to be barren as sea-shore which the tide has left, and containing but a mere handful of inhabitants. By such comparisons, by likening with bold sweeps of the brush the home geography to that in the territories of Kano, Damagarim, Damergou, and Aïr, we arrive at the conclusion that there would only be three towns throughout the length of England and Scotland, which we have called London, Sheffield, and Edinburgh for convenience of comparative distance at which they are set apart, and nothing intervening excepting a number of diminutive hut-villages of natives among the scrub-wood of the land. By this time, if your imagination has run free, you have shovelled the countless towns on the map of England, Scotland, and Wales into the sea, so that you have just the three you require and the requisite solitude surrounding them. But that is not all you do: trains must vanish, and ships that visit your shores, and the ocean around you shall be deserted, and no strangers shall come to the land. . . . Then is the picture of Solitude such as it is in the Western Sudan drawn to completion, and you may realise something of the ever-present weight of seclusion that hangs over ill-fated places that lie remotely out of the world and seem to soliloquise of Eternity, since they are so much alone and so near to the earth.

"Ah, it is a sad land!" is an exclamation I have oftentimes heard escape from the lips of Frenchmen who hold appointments in the country, for their vivacious natures feel most keenly the solitude of the barren land which envelops them with a grimness akin to the bare walls of a prison, and holds out no hope of escape until the date of release decreed, the while many a homesick heart has passionate longing for freedom of expression in convivial and comprehensive surroundings. I have been informed by officers that the depression of solitude—no doubt combined with the unnerving influence of malaria—is so great, that some men cannot stand it, and have to be prematurely sent from the territory in a state of total mental collapse; especially is this the case, it is asserted, among the N.C.O.s, who have naturally a narrower field of interest outside their military duties than the officers.

Zinder, like Kano, is surrounded with great earthen walls of similar height and strength, and they are so prominent that they may be sighted at a long distance off, whether you approach the place from the south or the north, for the nature of the landscape is such that you descend to Zinder (altitude 1,640 ft.) from the south, and look on its imposing bulwarks whenever you top a distant ridge which lies about two miles away; while you ascend to it from the north, where, perched on the crown of a rocky ridge, it has the pleasing appearance of a fortified castle. Kano has no view equal to this northern aspect of Zinder, which is of charming outline, and which looks particularly picturesque in the shades of evening, and fantastic in the moonlight, for then are the barren, unsympathetic surroundings almost forgotten under the softening influence of night's enchantment.

The site upon which Zinder stands is a curious one, insomuch that it is on a rising grade, which extends to the upper or most northern section of the town, which is on a low-rugged ridge extraordinary for the outcrop of giant boulders thereon, some of them many times the height of man, and lending an uncommon character to the surroundings of the habitations. The huts are built of clay-soil in the same manner as at Kano, for the community is, as there, largely Hausa, but the town in general, since it is smaller, is less bewildering in its narrow street-lanes, while there are markedly fewer inhabitants and less commotion. There is a circumstance in Zinder which is sad to relate: many of the dwellings are forsaken, and stand to-day in disrepair or in ruins, and a certain melancholy atmosphere of decline is there. Doubtless there are many causes for this decline, but those that are apparent and presently prominent are: firstly, that the lure of the rapidly ascending prosperity of industries and commerce of Kano has influenced many to desert the old town and go to settle in the great metropolis; and, secondly, that jurisdiction under military rule would appear to contain some element that is irksome to a certain number of natives, and so those who are not content, depart from under the immediate eyes of the administrative to seek, perhaps, a greater freedom in some distant bush-village, or in Hausaland in Nigeria. Natives of primitive environment are very easily influenced, and the act of changing abode an undertaking of small consequence, so that once a movement commences, others quickly follow the example of the leaders. My boys, Sakari and John, I fancy, expressed something of popular Hausa opinion when they quaintly proffered the conviction that "Kano is *sweet* past Zinder."

NATIVES DRAWING WATER AT BABAN TUBKI WELLS, ZINDER.

AMONG THE ROCKS OF ZINDER.

On the high ground just outside the western walls of Zinder there has sprung up, since the date of French occupation in 1900, an extensive European cantonment which is altogether modern and in strange contrast to the old town, to which it is distinctly foreign. Herein are the headquarters of the military administration of the Territoire Militaire du Niger. Here, laid out on broad lines, there are spacious buildings of creditable French colonial design—long flat-roofed, one-story bungalows in type, with pleasant balustrades that shelter cool verandas. The thick walls of the buildings are constructed by natives, with bricks which are baked with clay mud, obtained, strangely enough, by breaking into the ancient wall fortifications of Zinder, and kneaded, with the addition of fibrous straw, and baked or dried in the blazing sun. The domestic quarters or the administrative offices within the bungalows are delightfully cool, and it is pleasant indeed to have occasion to go inside out of reach of the hot sun of day which strikes down perpetually and without mercy on the scorched, expressionless sand of bare streets and compounds. (In the month of February the thermometer registers about 80° Fahr. in the shade at 8 a.m., and about 100° Fahr. at noon, although the hottest season is not reached until June and July.) The cantonment, which might almost be called a town within itself, is unique in the territory, there being nothing but outlying forts to compare with it; indeed, if we go outside it, not even the segregation at Kano, which contains about an equal number of Europeans, can compare, in my opinion, with the general planning and architectural appearance of Zinder. Which may be due to the fact that Kano is principally a township of trading stores, with domestic quarters overhead, whereas at Zinder there is not a shop in the place, and all the buildings are laid out on a well-conceived plan to accommodate the military administration, with due consideration to comfort and their exalted rank.

For the white traveller to come unawares upon the imposing buildings of Zinder, in such isolated surroundings, is naturally a great surprise, and a totally unexpected pleasure; and to the natives who arrive from the distant bush, or stop in the passing of their caravans, they must be a constant source of wonder.

In Zinder or in Kano, or, in fact, anywhere south of Aïr, you never hear "Zinder" given its official name, for, without exception, it is spoken of among the Hausa people under the designation of "Damagarim." Their explanation is that the name "Zinder" is not of Hausa origin, but is an old Arabic or Tamāshack name belonging to ancient rulers of northern race whose tribes have long ago been driven back, though the name still remains in use among the Semitic races in Aïr and other distant places on the old caravan routes to Tripoli and Algeria.

Zinder came under French rule in 1900.

It was in 1898 that large military missions were organised with the purpose of entering and occupying the country now known as the Territoire Militaire du Niger in the Western Sudan. The project was supported by a treaty between Britain and France which had been agreed on and signed in 1890—eight years before the undertaking was actually set afoot.

There was, in all, three separate missions, which started from Algeria, from the Niger river, and the Congo of French Equatorial Africa; and the scheme was that all would converge on Lake Chad, which was to be the rendezvous should each column meet with success. An object ultimately attained—and the Territoire Militaire was created in 1900, under the jurisdiction of a commandant, with headquarters established at

Zinder. In 1901 a second mission was organised to stabilise the position, and this mission was a powerful one in strength of arms, so that an imposing and awesome impression should be made on the minds of any disaffected native inhabitants, should such be encountered. During that year complete occupation of the Damagarim Region was peacefully carried out.

Below are statistics kindly furnished by the commandant, in September, 1920, of the native population in the region known as Damagarim, of which Zinder is the capital:—

Hausa	116.104
Beri-Beri	33,680
Fulani	5.969
Tuareg	1,520
Bellahs (Captive slaves and their descendants, of no caste)	4,564
Total Native Population	161,837

It will be seen that the Hausa race predominates, but the northern quarter of this region is near to the limit of their range, for they extend but little farther into the Damergou region, where they are only twenty-three thousand all told; and those principally in the neighbourhood of Tanout.

CHAPTER VI
THE SHORES OF BUSHLAND AND DESERT

Toward the end of February I left Zinder. Takoukout, 109 miles farther on, was to be my next camping-place.

Before leaving Zinder I heard plenty of discouraging news of the journey confronting me: exploits of armed robbers and great scarcity of food were freely spoken of, by both Europeans and natives, as existing drawbacks to visiting Aïr; and I began to note that my Hausa boys were growing restive and suspicious of what lay ahead. In fact, in the end those fearsome but idle rumours unsettled and unnerved Mona to such an extent that, when the time drew near to go forward, I decided to send him back to Kano, deeming it useless to take him further in such a state of mind. Sakari was little better, but he was so helpful in skinning, that I was loath to let him go, and by the aid of increased wages was able to induce him to continue.

It was the old familiar trouble, for I have always found it difficult to induce natives, most of whom appear to have a strong erratical and unreliable temperament in their composition, to leave their homes on a long journey, and, when possibilities of hunger and danger are added, trouble may be anticipated after the undertaking has commenced, no matter how auspicious the start, nor how binding the promises, which were perfectly sincere at the time they were made.

For my own part I had often puzzled over the question: "Why is it that Aïr has so long been avoided by naturalists and travellers?" for, so far as I could gather, no one had explored the country in British interests since Dr. Barth's geological and anti-slave trade mission to Central Africa in 1850—seventy years ago; but now I believed I had a cue, for hunger and danger are indeed companions of ill-omen sufficiently gruesome to warn away the wise—provided they are altogether without some opposite neighbours to stand by in time of stress and modify the fearsome picture. But of this more anon.

It may be said that in leaving Zinder, northward bound, one passes out into true Sahara and true wilderness. Henceforward the break-up of the natural bushland sets in, and wide belts of sand desert and dwarf bush alternate, until the vast sea of sand-plain is reached about 180 miles north of Zinder. Henceforward, also, the nature of the country undergoes change; it is more barren than before, which is reflected at once in the tremendous drop in population which occurs in the region or province of Damergou; and it is reflected, also, in the dwarf stature of the ill-nourished acacia trees, which, by the way, remind me much of the dying-down of the timber forests of Canada to the dwarf Scrub Pine on the shores of the sub-Arctic barren grounds. How strikingly similar are those two instances of landlocked shores, that are boundary between bushland and desert or plain, though they take effect in continents widely separated, and of entirely different climatic conditions! In both cases the trees are ill-thriven and dwarfed, but there is a difference: in the Sudan the cause is to be found in the unfertile sand and lack of moisture, while in Canada it is the severity of the winter in that particular latitude which lays its blight upon the land.

Then, too, as you enter wilderness and land of diminished population, you pass into country that is poorer in bird life, but richer by far in big-game than any territory to the south—as shall be seen as we progress.

The village of Tanout, 85 miles distant, lay across our path to Takoukout, and I set out with the intention of covering the distance in five days, which meant fairly stiff going for the well-loaded camels. As customary, we had the usual trouble with certain animals and their burdens on the first day out from Zinder, and were on the road, without pause for rest, from 7 a.m. till 4 p.m., when we reached Bakimaran after a journey of 18 miles. There is a belt of barren land which starts about 5 miles south of Zinder and continues northward until beyond Bakimaran—a belt altogether 25 to 30 miles in width—and it was across this that we travelled in setting out. It was drearily bare country, undulating in places with low rounded rises, sandy or covered with withered grass, and often with rough outcrops of gravel and boulders and rock, while, in patches, there was some scraggy bush and an odd tree. Few natives were encountered until Bakimaran was reached, and cattle and goat-herds, which are common to inhabited territory, were remarkably scarce, though the latter circumstance could, perhaps, in a measure be explained, as there are occasions in the dry season when grazing or water give out, and it is necessary that the main herds of the people be driven, often long distances, to find new pasturage. Apropos of this, there sometimes arises an amusing incident: a thunderstorm and sudden cloud-burst of heavy rain occurs in a limited locality and starts the grass growing green; before long a wandering bushman chances upon this fine pasture, and hastens away to fetch his lean and hungry herds to it; but on his return he finds to his disgust that someone, who has also made the discovery, has forestalled him, and there ensues lively dispute over rights of possession, which sometimes ends in angry abuse and even fighting—like to the madness of two hungry dogs that pounce together upon a dish of appetising food, antagonistic and snarling, although the vessel, in all probability, contains ample repast for both.

On the following day we departed from Bakimaran before dawn, and camped at Kaléloua in the afternoon. On the way we passed from the barren belt into fairly thick bush country, wherein no native habitations were seen until we reached our destination. The country now contained some big game. Red-fronted Gazelles were numerous, and were observed, usually, singly or in pairs, and I had no difficulty in shooting sufficient meat for my natives and the headmen of Kaléloua. Also one small band of giraffe were observed, but not disturbed, much to the disappointment of my natives, who were most anxious that I should kill those Rakuma-n-daji (Camels of the bush), which is the quaint Hausa name for those odd-shaped animals.

On the third day, which was a Sunday, we travelled to Dambiri. During the early part of the day we continued to pass through the bush belt we had entered on the previous day, but midway on the journey, after about 20 miles of bush country lay behind, this gave place again to open plains of sand and dry grass, which continued to Dambiri, and beyond as far as eye could see. In contour the open landscape was gently rolling, without any sharp rise, and not unlike the plain we had passed in leaving Zinder, except in the ever-growing supremacy of sand and solitude.

The growing poverty of the land is reflected in the natives and their habitations: the village of Dambiri, like the few others we had passed since leaving Zinder, was small, and the grass dwellings and yard fences built with less neatness and thoroughness than further south, and there was much that was unkempt and uncared for in the general aspect of the place, while the natives themselves were poor and raggedly clad. It is curious to note how surely the gradual change from fertile land to desert land is insistent of a corresponding falling off in the quantity and quality of the Hausaland natives, until they reach the very lowest ebb on the shores of the desert, and cease to venture farther; while another and vastly different race, the nomad Tuaregs, take up the duel of existence against nature in the great barren sea-like wastes beyond.

Dambiri, the designation of the village, is not an unpleasant Hausa name in quality of sound, but one gets rather a set-back if inquisitive enough to inquire into the literal English translation, for the meaning of the word is, "a bush cat with a bad smell"—which, I take it, rather pointedly has reference to the Civet Cat.

Once a week, on a set day, it is the custom of each village to hold market; and market-day constitutes the most important occasion in the routine of native life, for all are born traders, even in this impoverished territory of small productiveness, and outlying natives and the inhabitants of other villages travel eagerly, often long distances, with their quota of humble produce, to swell the concourse. Sunday was the day of market at Dambiri, so that there was unwonted stir about the place when we arrived, and much sound of tom-toms. I will not go into details of market-day at Dambiri, for the wares and proceedings are similar to those described at Kano; but I will make mention of the tom-tom music.

Those drum-beats which emanate so persistently from

the village, and which sound so monotonous and aimless to the European stranger, have in reality a definite purpose to the initiated, for they are in fact declaring urgent news that is intended to reach the ears of all, something after the manner of the old-fashioned town-crier in our own country, who goes forth with a hand-bell to make quaint public proclamations. Here are a few examples selected out of many: a certain rattan, or scale of beats, means that a beast (ox, sheep, or goat) is about to be killed, and that those who want fresh meat should hasten to purchase it before the excessive heat of the climate works destruction upon it; another sound denotes that meat is being sold at the market-place—not at the slaughter-place; others call the population to foregather before the King's dwelling, or to a wedding, or to feast; and yet another warns the people of the approach of a Saraki (local king) or a Amiru (emir or prince). In the examples which I have given, it will be seen that there is some need of urgency in the proclamation; and that is usually the case. Furthermore, the drum-beats of the tom-tom travel much farther than the human voice, and as it is often desired to reach the ears of the people at toil in the fields as well as those within the village, the inhabitants show cuteness in thus using their favourite instrument of music (?) for the duties of the day as well as for pleasure.

On the fourth day we journeyed throughout across strange wide plains of grass and sand, where no trees grow and but few scattered dwarf bushes, and camped at Mazia, which has an altitude of 1,700 ft., so that a decided ascent has set in since leaving Dambiri (1,500 ft.). In fact, on reaching Tanout next day, the highest altitude thus far encountered was recorded, namely, 1,800 ft., while a little further north, above Guinea Valley, the continuation of the same height of land recorded 1,900 ft., which is the highest point noted anywhere on my route from Kano to Agades.

During the late afternoon, at Mazia, I shot two Dorcas Gazelles and one great Arab Bustard to add to our scant supply of food. The dainty little Dorcas Gazelles are creatures that frequent the open plains and thin scrub, so that they too furnished evidence that we were now on the shores of the desert.

Water is not plentiful nor pure at Mazia: in fact, at this season (I am writing at the end of February), after four or five months have passed without rainfall, many wells reach a very low ebb, and pure water was a luxury enjoyed only at Zinder. Elsewhere it was always much discoloured with vegetable matter, and decaying timber props and soil; but it is precious enough even so, for it means no less than life to man and beast in this country of ravenous sunlight and terrifying dryness.

True to schedule, my caravan completed the 85-mile journey from Zinder to Tanout in the calculated time, and weary, dust-covered men and beasts camped at the Fort on the fifth day. On the way the country continued open and practically bushless, and little changed from that of the previous day, until the caravan drew near to Tanout, when three small hills became visible in the direction we were heading, while many of the low ridges among the sand-dunes were now strewn with dark glazed and rounded stones and pebbles, which gave to them a curious and striking resemblance, when viewed from a distance, to the colour of heather-hills at home in winter-time; also, in the low ground in the widely sweeping hollows between the rounded rises, there were often large circular or oval, basin-like, sand-coloured mud-flats, which, no doubt, hold lakes of water in the flood-rains of a good year (during some years very little rain falls in the wet season, which, roughly, is July and August in this territory, while there are occasions when the country is cruelly handicapped by two or three successive years of very slight rainfall), but which now appear to the eye as dry and smooth as a concrete area, and devoid of a single blade of grass or shrub or boulder—a cleanliness quite remarkable where no human hand has given aid.

At this season of the year Tanout is surrounded by dreadfully bare country, and one can scarcely conceive that the dead wastes of sand of the present time are, at another season, cultivated and green with the tall luxuriant growth of millet, guinea-corn, and maize; nevertheless, such is the case. The neighbourhood of Tanout is a renowned granary in the western Sudan, and it is to this territory that the Tuaregs of Aïr, who for lack of rain grow very little in their own country, send their caravans to barter for or purchase the grains which I have named above, which are the staple foods they live upon. This in some cases entails a journey of 170 miles (from Agades), and in others as much as 300 miles (from Timia, the furthest north inhabited village in Aïr to-day), which figures should be doubled if one wishes to calculate the full distance, outward and homeward, that caravans travel before they can bring food to the doors of their people.

The caravan track from the south runs straight into Tanout fort, which therefore acts as a barrier across the route, where all who pass may be questioned as to their identity and business—which is, in fact, a duty performed at this place, where a check is desired for military reasons on all native comings and goings. The fort, which stands facing south on a slight rise, is small; a square enclosure within high thick mud walls, containing a few humble hutments set back against the main structure and facing into the small open barrack square, which serve as quarters for the Europeans and magazines for military stores. The coloured troops are camped outside in a group of grass-thatched huts just west of the fort walls, where a straight avenue, planted with young trees that hesitate to take root in the ungracious soil, leads down to the native village, which lies in a dip about a quarter of a mile to the west. The native village is poorly constructed and primitive, much like the others in the region, even though this is the capital of Damergou. At the time of my visit there was one European officer and three N.C.O.s at the fort in command of the coloured troops; and a more isolated life than theirs could not well be imagined.

The native population in 1920 within the region of Damergou, of which Tanout is the capital, is detailed as follows:

Hausa	22,929
Beri-Beri	3,500
Tuareg	2,740
Fulani	370

Total Population 29,539

I also made some interesting notes with regard to the camels in this region and the alarming decline which has recently taken place—alarming because transport and existence in the country are so much dependent on those animals. It is stated that there were 15,000 camels in Damergou previous to the rising of 1916 in Aïr, whereas now there remain but 2,800—2,200 the property of Tuaregs, and 600 belonging to Beri-Beri. The chief reason of this great loss of animals appears to lie in the fact that at the time of the rising— which, I am told, had strong religious influence behind it, of the Senussi persuasion, as well as cunning instigation from Constantinople, where the Turks were already the sworn enemies of France in Europe—nearly all the Tuareg natives hastened north to join the rebel leader, Kaossen, taking with them their camels; and few of those camels ever returned. If one considers that a female camel has but one young at a birth, and that many years are required to rear camels to maturity, it will be seen that the loss is very serious, since it can hardly be replaced—unless animals were imported wholesale, which, I fancy, is an impossibility.

BERI-BERI BUSHMEN, DAMERGOU.

TANOUT VILLAGE.

In the following two days I completed the journey to my destination at Takoukout, which is merely the native name of a shallow valley, wherein a few nomad Tuaregs, who live in gipsy-like families, herding their cattle and goats and roaming from place to place in the virgin bush, have excavated numerous pit-like wells to obtain sufficient water for themselves and their stock.

There are no native villages north of Tanout— none until Agades is reached, 169 miles away, at the southern end of the mountains of Aïr.

There is no water anywhere between Tanout and Takoukout at this season, so, before setting out, one camel was loaded with goat-skins of water sufficient to serve for the journey.

The country north of Tanout is very irregular, with much of the ground surface strewn with pebbles and bare of vegetation, while some strange and picturesque escarpments were passed before descending into Guinea Valley, which is about 300 ft. below the level of the high land on which Tanout is situated. In Guinea Valley, 13 miles north of Tanout, the barren belt, which had first been entered beyond Kaléloua at a point 50 miles back, is left behind, and in the low ground there is now more bush-growth, which continues to Takoukout, and beyond to the very edge of the desert-sea.

After a pleasant cool journey by moonlight, my caravan reached Takoukout on the second morning after my departure from Tanout; whereupon I prepared to make a permanent encampment whence to do some hunting, for in this last belt of bush before the desert is entered there is much game reported, and, what concerned me most, ostriches! Lord Rothschild was particularly anxious to secure specimens of those birds from this isolated region.

CHAPTER VII
OSTRICH HUNTING

IT is remarkable that in the wide range of territory over which I journeyed, ostriches were to be found only in one particular part. I have endeavoured to show, in the preceding chapter, that on the shores of the desert there are alternating strips of barren desert and bushland, and it is in the very last belt of bush, which reaches to the actual edge of the desert, that ostriches are to be found— roughly between the small forts of Tanout and Aderbissinat in a scattered bush belt about 80 miles in width. I have seen one ostrich track within 30 miles of Agades (near Tegguidi cliff) and some 50 miles north of the usual range, while I have heard reports of ostriches being near Agades, but in actual experience I have seen enough to feel satisfied that they do not often range far beyond the bush belt, which dies out a short distance north of Aderbissinat, and about 80 miles south of Agades, which is near to the foot of the Aïr mountains.

In deciding to make camp at Takoukout, I had selected the place put forward by my camel-men and by the local natives as the most favourable for the pursuit in view, while at the same time they warned me that ostriches were not numerous anywhere in the country; and their judgment eventually proved to be quite sound.

It was March 4th when I reached Takoukout and set about preparing a permanent camp. I had had an escort of Senegalese soldiers with me since leaving Zinder, for it is the military rule that no European shall proceed north of that point unaccompanied by an armed escort, and from Tanout six soldiers were detailed to go with me to guard my belongings and person at Takoukout, so that on this occasion pitching camp was rather an elaborate business, as it required some defensive arrangement. With the purpose of gaining a little shade, a clump of bush in a slight hollow was selected, and there camp was established within a thick brushwood barricade of thorn bushes, which was erected all around the encampment for protection and as an enclosing wall. It was difficult to find any local natives to help in cutting down trees for hut construction, since the few that existed within visiting distance of the Takoukout wells were hidden away in solitary bush-camps, and it was difficult, also, to secure grass in the neighbourhood sufficiently long for the purpose of covering in the walls and roof of the huts; but a few Tuaregs of the district came to our aid on the second day, and a comfortable camp was knocked into shape in due course. There were then within the zareba: my tent erected for my own use; a grass-hut workshop; a small cooking shelter for John; and, set some distance apart, four rough hut sun-shelters for the soldiers, as well as for Sakari, a local hunter, and a camel-man; while my horse, and those belonging to escort, and two camels for carrying water-skins or game on long journeys in the bush, were also within the enclosure on nights that I happened to be there.

A notable addition to my personnel at this time was a native hunter, of whom I shall make brief reference. This local warrior, whose proper name was Dirto, but whom my followers invariably called Tsofo (old man), was secured for me by the French officer at Tanout, so that I would have a man familiar with hunting, and, above all, familiar with the puzzling sameness of the level seas of low bush-forest which prevailed in the Takoukout region.

Tsofo, as I too called him, since the name fitted so well, had the reputation of being a great *chasseur* who had lived his life hunting the wild animals of the bush with snare and bow and arrows, which primitive devices are the only ones available to the natives for pursuit of the chase in the country.

For the purpose of hunting, and, particularly as a means of defence, bows and arrows are universally in use in Damergou, and an adult male native is seldom seen abroad, no matter on what business he is intent, without bow in hand and a leather sheath, containing usually about fifteen arrows, slung from a cord over the left shoulder. The same weapon is much used in Damagarim and Kano provinces, but not to the same extent as in this still more remote and exposed zone, where the need for an arm for protection is imperative, since among the natives there is not only lingering dread of robbers descending across the desert from the north, but also the wild instinct of very primitive people, in dreadfully primitive surroundings, to wage war, one against the other, under the grim impulse of an existence that demands self-protection before all else, and upholds the faith that life is a struggle for "the survival of the fittest." The European law of the country forbids any natives to possess fire-arms.

But, to return to Tsofo, I will endeavour to describe him, for he was an odd character in appearance and constitution, and at the same time somewhat typical of many of his kind. When I first laid eyes on him, I could not believe that the ill-clad, unkempt creature that stood before me was the chosen hunter that was to accompany me. Upon my word, I never saw a dirtier native; his bit of a gown, once white, now a smoked blackish colour, was cast carelessly over his shoulder and hung in rags about him, full of rents and badly frayed round the bottom edge; beneath this he wore an equally discoloured buck-skin loin-cloth and apron. He carried not a scrap of food when he joined me, and had nothing about his person except bow and arrows, and a hatchet and hunting-knife of his own crude making. Undoubtedly he was past his prime, in fact he was an old man, despite the stalwart framework that remained of deep chest, and mighty thighs and lower limbs which bespoke an athlete. His face was so wrinkled with exposure, and with frowning beneath the fierce rays of the sunlight, and so unkempt that it would be unkind to estimate his character by it. The coarse hair on his head and the scrub-beard on his chin were almost entirely grey, and his watery red-rimmed eyes betrayed declining years.

He wore a broad-brimmed, high-crowned hat, locally woven with dyed grasses, which was not unlike the garish headgear of a Spanish muleteer. On his feet he wore rough sandals cut to shape from a single piece of thick antelope-hide. He was a Beri-Beri native of a very primitive class, and most of his kind that I have seen have fine physique, but coarse features of heavy unattractive type, and I have often doubted the purity of their breeding.

As I have said, it would be unkind to judge Tsofo's character by his unprepossessing appearance, so I will tell you how I found him in daily life. In his favour be it said: he knew perfectly the bush country where we hunted, and, during many long journeys in the most difficult bush I have ever encountered, he never failed to find his way back to the base camp, though he had one or two occasions for anxiety. On the other hand, Sakari, the Hausa boy, was quite bewildered in this country, and got separated from us and lost on three occasions, which goes to show that all natives have not that marvellous faculty of travelling in a given direction with animal-like instinct and memory, which is usually their most striking gift. On account of this shortcoming, it is interesting to note that Sakari had lived most of his life in Lagos and Kano, and belonged to a family of shop-keepers, so that no doubt environment, which has such a powerful influence on the character of mankind as well as on the lesser creatures of the earth, had much to do with his loss of natural instinct.

Tsofo's knowledge of the bush was his greatest asset; as a hunter he was not a success, for undoubtedly he was too old, as I will explain below. But he was most eager to serve me and to bag game, and spared no pains to that end. Also he was on friendly terms with the few nomad Tuaregs who came about the shallow wells at Takoukout to water their herds and fill their water-skins. (With them this old hand at travelling light and camping anywhere bartered part of his share of the buck-meat killed, so that he could have millet-meal (*Dawa*) and goat cheese (*Chuku*) to vary his diet.) He was kindly disposed to all he met, and had always a word and a hand-pat for children, while he never attempted that domineering attitude which natives are so prone to assume, when backed by a white man's presence, to bully some gift from the frightened bush-people.

Being an old man, long days were too much for Tsofo, but, even so, he never dropped behind while he hunted, though the efforts of the day often caused him to groan with pain and complain of sickness when we got into camp at night. He had wonderful strength and endurance for his age, and I often found myself admiring his dogged gait, though it was nothing less than pure animal toughness of the kind which one associates with tramps, or tinkers in the old country, who live outdoors the year round, and care little for bodily comfort and cleanliness so long as they can secure enough to eat.

Tsofo had his limitations: he would eat food in almost any condition and in large improvident quantities. When he joined my caravan he was well-nigh in a starving condition, and when a gazelle was killed for food, the old man fell upon it like a jackal, starting on the raw entrails, when disembowelling the animal, and thereafter cooking and eating meat until he was completely gorged. Next day he was sick and not so greedy, but he soon recovered, and before long I knew him to be a savage, untamed glutton when he had food in his possession. The old rascal, I'm sure, had been a very fine hunter and tracker, for he knew all the "tricks of the trade," as it were, and the habits of the animals; but both eyesight and hearing were impaired to such an extent that he altogether lacked the acutely keyed keenness of those senses, which are essential to good hunting. I soon found that he was a blunderer after he had spoilt a chance or two to shoot in failing to detect the first slight movement of wary game, while he proved a dreadfully slow tracker, because, by reason of his bad eyesight, he often overshot the footprints he was following in the sand, and had to search about to pick up the right track again. His knowledge of the bush was invaluable, and, besides, he had an unassuming character that pleased me, so I always took him out, but when I understood his weakness, I did not allow him to join me up in front, but bade him follow some hundred yards behind.

Before I proceed to deal with the actual search for ostriches, I feel I should make reference to the climate, and its fierce antagonism to comfortable hunting in this part of the world.

I would not like to boldly assert that the climate in the

Western Sudan is unhealthy for Europeans, for such an assertion might appear unjust in the estimation of some men of very adaptable and robust constitution, but on the whole I think it can justly be said that the climate is such as belongs to Central Africa in general, and that therefore it already has an accepted reputation for being very hot and trying. North of the neighbourhood of Kano there is no open water or marsh in the dry season (approximately from October to July), so that for the greater part of the year no hanging dampness, no mosquitoes, and no malaria are experienced in the country with which I am dealing—which is so much to the good. On the other hand you have a mighty opponent to comfort and health in the form of the merciless sun, which glares down upon the white glittering sand-surface of the earth with unmitigated fierceness, laying an awesome withering breathlessness upon the land which saps the energy of man and beast, so that they perforce forsake their occupations for the greater part of the day and seek rest in the shade; while even the plant life cannot survive the remorseless moisture-consuming oppressor in the sky, and leaves and grass that were green in the short rainy season, lie wilted and bleached on the sand. We Europeans of temperate zones love the sun, but I'm afraid Old Sol is a graceless and greedy robber of the earth's vitality in some climes, and here, where Nature has raised no compact leafy screen upon the land, nor sends not clouds across the sky, he well-nigh reigns supreme over smitten wastes that lie wretchedly subdued because of his unopposed power. On account of the intense heat, and the exhaustion resultant therefrom, I found the climate very trying at times, for there are many occasions when the hunter must be afoot all day in the open, while, even if he chances to be in camp, the collector seldom enjoys relaxation from his busy labours by the specimen bench during the valuable hours of daylight. Records of temperature on 27th March read: 7 a.m., 58% Fahr.; noon, 105% Fahr.; 8 p.m., 71% Fahr. I have brought up the subject of climate at this juncture, because it was at Takoukout that I felt the heat more trying than at any other period—in fact, it temporarily sapped my strength to such an extent that I came near collapsing under the strain of day after day searching the stifling hot waterless country for restless, ever-travelling ostriches.

I will not enter into every incident of the unlucky hunting that I experienced at Takoukout, but will quote from my diary a few records of typical days. In all I hunted twenty days for ostriches and saw sixteen birds, *but never fired a shot at any of them*. Nevertheless, the general details of hunting them are, I feel sure, not without peculiar interest, and on that account I am induced to give some personal experiences.

7th March.—Away hunting all day. Left camp 6.30 a.m.; returned 5.30 p.m. Set out north-west till noon, then north till 3 p.m., then south-east to camp. Searched again for ostriches without seeing any; a few tracks encountered, all leading westward. In late afternoon, having seen no ostriches, I decided to break the silence, which I was particular to preserve so long as there was hope of coming on any of the great wary birds, and to shoot gazelle, if the opportunity offered when nearing camp. Now, the country within the last bush-belt is rich in game, and a day never passed without seeing some beautiful gazelle-creatures which surely must rank among the most noble on earth, so delicate in form are they, so superbly graceful, so joyously alive in activity and in the sheen of health that casts a glamour over their soft rich coats, so proud with their finely poised heads and large inquiring eyes and nostrils. There were three species of them: sometimes dainty little Dorcas Gazelles, pale fawn in colour, like the dry grass and sand, would be encountered in small lots of two, four, and five, and occasionally in herds of about ten to fifteen in the open sandy glades, which they seem to prefer to frequent; sometimes, again, the rich rufous Red-fronted Gazelles would be seen among the acacias, usually single, in pairs, or in threes and fours—never in herds; while yet again the big and striking Dama Gazelles would be encountered—striking because of the large amount of conspicuous white which they possess. They are the largest species of the genus. They were occasionally seen single, but are much given to associate in herds of ten, twenty, thirty, or more. (Later on, in August, after the advent of the Rains, which had caused a tall rank grass to spring up in the bush and gave leaf to the acacias, so that the country appeared much more enclosed and vastly changed from the open barrenness which it possessed in the dry season, those animals appeared to be migrating northward out into the desert margin; no doubt so that they might breathe the wind of the open places, and be to some extent free from flies, and feed on the fresh delicate grasses that were then sprouting forth. On one notable day, when between Tegguidi and Abellama—before the bush belt is entered when journeying from the north—I passed herd after herd of Dama Gazelles, and was able to get close enough on three occasions to count the numbers. The totals were 37, 44, and 84, and in each case I probably overlooked a few.

YOUNG OSTRICHES.

DORCAS GAZELLE.

The local Hausa names of those three species are: Dorcas Gazelle, *Matakundi*; Red-fronted Gazelle, *Barewa*; Dama Gazelle, *Mena*, sometimes *Myna*. The Hausa for ostrich is *Jimmina*.

From the above may be gathered some idea of buck we expected to see on this evening of which I am writing; true, there were other kinds, but so rarely seen that, as a general rule, they could be discounted, though their clean-cut tracks in the sand were occasionally crossed. As far as my observations go, those others were White Oryx, Korrigum, and Giraffe.

We were still a fair distance from camp when a nice herd of a dozen Dama Gazelles were sighted, and, after a certain amount of running and dodging to keep a screen of bush cover between the herd and myself, I got a good view of them, and managed to drop the animal that appeared to have the best head. I got another as they jumped and paused to ascertain from which direction the danger threatened, and yet another in following them up a little way; for, besides wanting specimens, meat was needed in camp for all the natives—fresh meat and sun-dried. One of the animals was a splendid male, but, as so often happens, the fine head was spoilt through one horn being slightly deformed and broken at the tip. However, one female was a good specimen, and, as both sexes were desirable, I reserved it for a museum specimen, and told the natives not to cut it in any way. The other two were disembowelled, and all were then loaded on to the two camels that had come up from the rear, where they had been following unseen. The day was then drawing to a close, but incident was not yet finished with, for, before reaching camp, I stalked and shot a Red-fronted Gazelle—also a nice museum specimen— and missed its companion.

8th March.—In camp all day skinning and preserving two gazelles, one jackal, and a few small birds.

9th March.—Left camp at daybreak to continue search for ostrich. Travelled eastward. Made short halt at 10 a.m. Nothing, so far, has been seen of our quarry, though four tracks of yesterday's making were crossed—three of them leading in a southerly direction and one in northerly direction. Five Dorcas Gazelles seen about time of halting. Continued on the move after a brief consultation with Tsofo, at the same time changing direction more into the north, and soon entered country where bush was more plentiful, for previously it had been very open and the scrub thin. But up to noon-time nothing seen moving; sun blazing hot. Lunched and lay watchful for a time in the doubtful shade of a poor-leaved tree, while the natives slept.

Resumed search through bush about 2 p.m., about which time some Dama Gazelles were seen resting in the heat of day. Those animals were given a wide berth and left undisturbed, as is my unvarying custom when the search for ostrich is afoot. In my opinion, to disturb any such game which, for the time being, happen to be of secondary interest, and set them hurrying away before you in alarm, is almost as bad as to lose patience and fire an unimportant shot, for in both cases you stand to spoil the great chance you hope for, since there is always the possibility of giving warning to the creatures you seek, and which may at any moment be at hand all unknown to the hunter.

Close on 4 p.m. we came upon a very fresh ostrich track where a bird had passed about two hours earlier in the afternoon. Followed track some distance, but bird not seen, and gave up, as there appeared no prospect of overtaking it before darkness set in; indeed, so far as that was concerned, there was no certainty that it would be overtaken even in a whole day's travelling, for they are birds that are incessantly moving on from place to place, while, if alarmed, they run long distances before assured that they are safe from their enemies.

Leaving the ostrich tracks, we started on a long wearisome journey in a westerly direction to camp, while the sun set and the day finished. I and the natives—Sakari, Tsofo, and the man with the camels—showed much relief and gladness when at last, after the trying labour of picking our way over rough unfamiliar country in the dark, we caught the welcome light of our camp-fires, beckoning from afar; and we were safely back in camp an hour and a half after dark.

From what I have thus far seen, added to local information gleaned from more than one quarter, I am satisfied that ostriches are far from plentiful in this isolated strip of country that they inhabit, and it has been, and will continue to be, hard hunting to secure the desired specimens— long arduous days of tracking through the sand-swept bush, beneath the inextinguishable sun, until one day, perchance, we meet across each other's tracks. Tsofo, the old native hunter, claims that for a number of years hunting conditions within the territory have been undergoing change owing to the influx of nomad Tuaregs, with their herds of goats and cattle, from the neighbourhood of Aïr. Those natives in small numbers are now scattered about in the bush at distant intervals, and, possibly, if they were sedentary, no harm would be done, but the necessity of constantly changing to fresh ground, so that enough food may be found for their herds, and their own strong nomadic instincts, lead those Tuaregs to range from place to place continually and disturb considerable areas, and Tsofo rightly claims that this circumstance greatly tends to frighten any timid game such as the ostrich, for nothing is more disturbing to their keen senses than to come across the tainted trail which clumsy herds of domestic animals invariably leave behind wherever they happen to pass, or pause in feeding. Tsofo declares, and no doubt there is a lot of truth in his statement, that when the French occupied Agades (the first French military mission visited Agades in 1904), some of the wild unenthralled Tuaregs of Aïr fled from the country in fear of the invaders and scattered broadcast on the edge of the desert as far south as the neighbourhood of Tanout in their secretive, gipsy-like wanderings.

10th March.—Hunting as unfruitful as yesterday.

11th March.—Almost at dark, after a long uneventful tramp through the bush, I at last sighted ostrich. Crossing from a bare open glade, and approaching quite close to an edge of fairly thick bush, I suddenly stood motionless in my stride, for I had seen the head and neck of an ostrich just within the cover. The acacias awkwardly blocked further view, and breathlessly I made a short careful creep forward. When I rose, inch by inch, to peer forward, I found I was quite close to a great black male ostrich, but, unfortunately, it stood on the far side of a tree, and the trunk and all intervening branches and foliage hid it to such an extent that I could not discern head from tail, nor where to place a fatal shot. Therefore I tried to change my position very slightly, and was in the act of doing so, when, of a sudden, another bird on my right, a grey hen which I had not seen amongst the bushes nor thought of guarding against, rushed off in alarm, startling the bird I was stalking and two others. In an instant, almost, they were out of sight among the bushes, and although I rushed forward hoping that an open space was not far ahead and that

I would get a shot at them making off, I had no such luck, and never saw them again. My disappointment was acute, the more so because I had plenty of time to fire from the first position, after crawling forward, if I had foreseen what was to follow, and taken the risk of getting a lucky shot home.

Who that is a sportsman does not know disappointment of the kind? I fancy we all do, and, moreover, have been lured on to stick to many a difficult quest in once having seen and let escape some much-prized quarry. Does not the fisherman who has risen a nice fish and missed it, after many patient hours on the water, go on thereafter with a new zest and a brighter outlook? It was so in my case; and, instead of returning to Takoukout, and having sufficient water on the camels, we camped out in the bush this night with a new excitement, and hoping to make amends on the morrow.

12th March.—Camped comfortably overnight.

Hopes awakened by yesterday's experience doomed to disappointment, for the day's hunting brought no reward. Returned to camp in the afternoon; very tired, for the sun and the glittering sand take it out of one. The sun seems to hold its fatiguing intensity from 9 a.m. till 4 p.m. at this time of year.

A number of gazelles seen, and tracks in the sand are constantly crossed. It is splendid country for tracking, and most interesting to read and study the signs upon the smooth sand.

Sand covers the whole earth in this country, and reminds me much of a land of snow. The level wastes, that are random planted with wiry, hard-living thorn trees (acacias), have patches that are wind-swept and crusted to hardness underfoot, and there are soft driftings in the slight declivities and about the plant roots, while the grass is so scant in most places, that the few blades that stand have the aspect of such as peep above the surface of a country that has been the victim of a deep fall of snow.

13th March.—A day in camp. Feeling somewhat overstrained. Skinned birds all forenoon; collected ten more in afternoon. Giving bush a rest in hope that I'll have more luck next outing.

14th March.—Greater part of day skinning eleven birds. Toward evening made short hunt to secure meat for camp, and had a few shots at gazelle, wounding two, but failed to get either of them. I shot badly: possibly through being overtired.

When about to turn home, I stood on a slight elevation and looked out across a wide shallow hollow on to an open grass slope similar to the one I occupied, and carefully scanned the distant view, more from habit than in hope of seeing anything of particular interest. My surprise was therefore manifest to the natives with me when I discovered four black-looking objects, like boulders or small dark shrubs, in the far distance, that moved and were undoubtedly ostriches. In an instant the blacks were beside me imbued with excitement equal to my own as I pointed out the birds. Immediately, for receding day threatened to frustrate this lucky chance, I started on a long encircling stalk, since the birds were in an open position that was difficult to approach unseen, and great care had to be exercised, for ostriches are endowed with wonderfully keen eyesight. Unfortunately, when I cast in toward the position of the quarry, I saw nothing, and thought I had misjudged the place and was a little too high on the slope. I then cast lower down, but with no better result, and soon picked up their tracks leading westward on to the summit of the rise. Perhaps I had been heard by the birds, for pebbles crunched annoyingly underfoot in places, or perhaps they had merely shifted onward in feeding; I could not tell, for I had been out of sight of them almost since the stalk began. They might still be quite close; but that availed me nothing, for the moments of daylight, that had been precious, were finished. So there was nothing for it but to give up and return to camp empty-handed.

15th March.—Left camp at daybreak, taking with me two mounted native escort, two camels and camel-men, Tsofo, and Sakari in charge of my horse. I usually have a horse following behind in case it should be required in an emergency, but never use it in actual hunting, for the hoofs resound over loudly for my liking, and I prefer to be far out ahead of all following, excepting one native gun-bearer, and, on foot, moving along as quietly as possible. I took a larger following than usual on this occasion, and camels to carry skins of water, as I intended to be away some days.

Travelled all day in north-westerly direction, but no ostriches seen, and only two single tracks of them were crossed.

At dusk shot one gazelle for food, and camped at the kill for the night.

Gazelle continue to be constantly seen. I have noted that Dama Gazelles have a remarkable tendency to run up-wind when alarmed, an impulse so strong that if you know this habit, and make to get nearly between them and the wind, instead of making directly for them, they will almost certainly pass you as they run away. As a general rule they are very alert animals, and more difficult to stalk than either the Red-fronted or Dorcas Gazelles.

16th March.—Moved on again at daylight, first heading westward, then swinging more into the north under the direction of Tsofo, making for a well on the Agades trail named

Tchingaraguen, so that the horses could be watered and the water-skins refilled. During the morning oryx and giraffe tracks were seen on the sand, which were the only incidents of note. Oryx tracks were not uncommon, but giraffe tracks were seldom seen during my wanderings through this bush. Neither animal was important to my collections, so that I did not attempt to follow their tracks.

We reached Tchingaraguen about 11 a.m., and made short halt while I breakfasted and the horses were watered—the poor brutes were desperately thirsty. This half-barren, shadeless sand country is not a land for horses, and they suffer a lot from the heat, while fodder is miserably poor. I have resolved that when I move on to Agades I will leave my horse behind at Tanout and henceforth ride a camel.

Leaving Tchingaraguen, we crossed the Agades track and held south-east. In other words, we had reached the crown of the huge circular trail we were making through the country, with the starting-point at Takoukout; we had covered the western side of that circle, and had now the eastern side to trace in on the way homeward. The country we entered, once well clear of the watering-place, held more encouraging signs than hitherto, for a fair number of footprints were seen upon the sand, sometimes where an ostrich had passed, sometimes where birds had been feeding on the bleak acacias or on a little patch of living ground weed; once, too, I came upon the "form" where a bird had recently had a sand-bath, and picked up a few feathers which had dropped out while the bird rolled in the dust. But they are birds that are ever on the move, here one hour and gone the next; and this day I never sighted a bird.

There is at least one substantial reason at the present time for the restless wanderings of the ostrich, while I am not at all sure that it does not account for their scarcity of numbers for the time being in the territory. It was Tsofo who first drew my attention to the marked scarcity of ostrich food. Time and again the old man, who knew this country like a book, though he had not hunted in it for more than a year back, led me to places where he knew, from past experience, that there should be good feeding-ground for the birds. But always when we got to these chosen places where their favourite plants were expected to be abundant, he would look sadly about him, for the bushes were almost as bare as dead trees, and scarcely a plant grew on the soil that was not burnt up. The good old fellow at such times bravely held his tongue, so that he would not dishearten me, unaware that it was easy to detect his disappointments and make one's own deductions. It was not difficult to see that the growth was suffering from a water-famine, and when at last I taxed Tsofo on the poor state of the country, he confessed his surprise at finding it in such condition, and said that the cause must lie in the fact that no plentiful rain fell in the territory last year. At a later date I happened to learn that at Agades in the same year—1919— small rainfall had occurred only on two days, and there is little doubt that there was a similar drought further south, and that Tsofo spoke the truth.

But nevertheless it is difficult to conceive that a land, where so fierce a sun is dominant, can survive without rainfall for almost two years (sometimes, the natives declare, they experience drought for so long as three years in succession), and it is little wonder that, with such grim set-backs to existence, the ground is largely barren and the bush-growth stunted.

But that the plants of the earth do not always survive, I can vouch for, for when I passed east of the mountains of Tarrouaji in Aïr later in the year, I saw there a belt of standing acacia bush, on the edge of mountain and desert, that was quite dead, and to all appearance from no other cause than from lack of nourishment. It was an eerie sight and a desolate one: every bush dead, the limbs colourless and lifeless, and the bark hanging therefrom in shreds—a graveyard, where the struggle for existence had been greater than could be withstood.

It was not difficult to ascertain which plants the ostriches fed on at the season I was hunting them, for one could tell by the tracks in the sand exactly where a bird stopped in the act of feeding, while careful survey of the foliage further revealed where pieces had been broken off. I brought home those plants that were known to me as food of the ostrich so that they might have authoritative identification, and I give some notes on them herewith; while I am indebted to Dr. A. B. Rendle, of the British Museum, for their scientific names:

1. *Cassia* nr. *obovata* (Leguminosæ) Hausa: Filasko. "Senegal Senna." A small low shrub, with yellow flowers and short flat pods, which curve in a quarter circle and have a raised saw-edged rib down their centre. The local natives claim this plant to be the one most sought after by ostriches.

2. *Cucumis* sp. (Cucurbitaceæ) Hausa: Gurji. A small ground-creeping gourd, which has often long-reaching trailers. Ostriches feed on the leaves of this plant.

3. *Mœrua rigida* R. Br. (Capparidaceæ) Hausa: Chichiwa. A small tree, with white flowers and tiny elongated leaves.

4. *Oxystelma bornouense* R. Br. (Asclepiadaceæ) Hausa: Hanjin Rago. A slender, climbing creeper, which flourishes in the topmost branches of acacia trees, there overreaching and

having green foliage in a thick cluster. When trees are almost bare of leaves, as often is the case in the dry season, the clumps of green of this parasite in the tree-tops are conspicuous and easy to find, which is perhaps a kind provision of Nature, so that the creatures who seek such food may be guided to it from afar. The leaves of the plant contain considerable juice, and it is the second favourite food of the ostrich; while it is also a rich titbit for camels, who are very fond of it.

Native hunters of the territory know those plants well, and utilise the knowledge to secure the downfall of many an ostrich; for it is where they expect birds to feed that they conceal the traps that are the only means by which they can capture them, for ostriches are too wary to be shot with bow and arrow. The ostrich trap is of the same kind as that which the natives use for antelope (and for wild sheep in Aïr), but it is of a much larger size and stronger. It is constructed in this way: two wands about the thickness of half an inch are relaxed in hot water and bent into the form of a complete circle which has a diameter of 14 in.; those rods are bound at their meeting points, and allowed to dry and set in the form of a rigid hoop, whereupon they are laid together, while closely grouped hard unbending straws, about the length of a pencil, are inserted between them and stoutly bound in place with strips of bark; all the straws radiate to the inside centre, but do not quite meet, so that, though they are held firmly on the circular frame, they have no support whatever where they converge in the centre, therefore the finished article is a flat tray of rigid straws, which is firm around the rim, but is subject to collapse outward in the centre if any great weight be put upon it. The contrivance looks a simple enough thing, but there is more in the construction than first appears. The trap is for ostrich, and on that account it is desirable that smaller animals shall not "spring it," and the resourceful hunters have hit on the solution to a nicety, simply by increasing the thickness and rigidity of the straws, so that they will give beneath the weight of an ostrich, while they will remain undisturbed beneath the footstep of a gazelle.

To set an ostrich trap, a hole is excavated in the sand, say, beneath an acacia thorn, which bears an attractive cluster of the plant *Oxystelma bornouense*, and exactly where it is anticipated a bird will stand that is intent on reaching the choice foliage; this hole is 10 to 12 in. in diameter, so that when the straw tray is laid over it, the greater part of the surface lies over the cavity, while the rim is firmly held on the edge of the pit. When the tray is in position, a very strong noose made out of plaited raw-hide thongs, and opened to a diameter similar to the rim of the tray, is laid over it, and the end attached to a stout log: this log is buried beneath the sand, while the tray and noose are also concealed by smoothing the sand surface over them until every sign of disturbance of the soil is obliterated. If an ostrich chance to visit the place, and approaches to feed on the small clump of green leaves, with his eyes fixed upon the coveted morsel, he will almost certainly step upon the concealed tray; whereupon his foot breaks through it into the hole, and the noose jumps upward and is around the limb when the unfortunate bird hurriedly withdraws the foot from the hole. Thus he is caught; snared so securely that, powerful bird though he is, he has no hope of breaking loose. He will yet go a long distance, but trailing the log behind him, and leaving the tell-tale marks of it in the sand wherever he goes—and his captors will find him in the end.

17th March.—Off again at daylight. But first searched for a Dama Gazelle which I had wounded at camp almost at dark on the night before, and had been unable to find it. Almost where we had given up tracking it on the previous night we found the animal's deathbed, but only pools of blood-discoloured sand, and some green grazings from the stomach, so completely had the animal been devoured in the night by jackals and hyenas. I wanted to find the head, for I thought it was a very fine one when shooting at the animal, and I had all the natives search the neighbourhood of the kill. But so complete had been the meal of the night-prowlers, that not a vestige of anything was found except one solitary piece of shoulder-blade.

To-day travelled south-east, but in morning nothing seen except gazelle. However, about 10 a.m., advancing cautiously over a low ridge, I saw at last a single ostrich; but the sharp-eyed brute saw me at the same time also, and cleared right away, very wild. The sun was now blazing hot, but we had to keep going incessantly, as the water-skins were almost empty, and we had a long way to go to reach Takoukout before sundown.

About noon again sighted ostriches—three of them away to the west in fairly open country. Made long stalk, keeping out of sight in the slight hollows, but could not overtake the birds, as they were moving too rapidly; followed them a long way, but finally had to give up. Throughout the remainder of the day no more birds were seen, and we reached Takoukout at sundown, after being three days in the bush, and having seen, in that time, but four ostriches, distant and wild. Very glad to get into camp; our water was finished, and all were very done up with the excessive heat. The poor horses drank till I thought they would collapse.

20th and 21st March.—Two fruitless days hunting for ostrich. Not a bird seen. Travelled north, then west to Eleki, and returned to camp on second day. Brought back one Dama Gazelle, two Dorcas Gazelles, one partridge, and four small specimens.

I have endeavoured to give an idea of hard hunting in a dreary belt of country, and beneath a pitiless sun, where the reward desired was withheld to the bitter end. It is a chapter of adversity, such as we all meet at some time or other in our experiences of life, but may still hold some value, even although the chief pursuit devolved in failure.

CHAPTER VIII
LEAVING THE BUSHLAND BEHIND: AÏR ENTERED

ON 29th March my Takoukout camp was dismantled, and everything packed up in readiness to continue farther on into the interior, where Agades, in Aïr, I hoped would be my next place of halt.

My stay at Takoukout had been the least profitable of camping places. It is true it was not territory where bird life was plentiful, but results would have been better if ostrich hunting had not taken up the greater part of my time.

At this date my total collections numbered 485 birds and 121 mammals, as well as 374 butterflies and 138 moths; and, of those, 58 birds were taken at Takoukout and 8 mammals, including three complete gazelles (not merely the head and horns, but the whole animal).

At the end of my stay at Takoukout I lost the services of Sakari. He had grown less and less inclined to follow the arduous life I led him, whilst he had developed a hankering to be back amongst the companionship of his own people. Moreover, he had now a better idea of the stern conditions which the nature of the country imposed—conditions that promised to grow worse rather than better—and plainly he did not relish the prospect of what lay ahead. His three experiences of being lost in the bush, which I refer to in the preceding chapter, did not tend to help matters, and, finally, seeing that his heart was no longer in his work, I considered it advisable to pay him off and send him back, though I was very sorry to lose him, since his departure left me without any one to assist in the task of skinning specimens.

I bid good-bye, also, to the old hunter Tsofo, who had joined me for the period that I hunted at Takoukout, so that I might have the assistance of his local knowledge. He had never been to Aïr, and, therefore, could not aid me in the same way further on; a circumstance which I think we both regretted, for the old fellow was genuinely loath to go home, and I sorry to lose him. There had always been plenty of buck-meat in camp, and the old fellow had never wanted food, which was a state of affairs that greatly pleased him, for he had close acquaintance with poverty in the ordinary round of living in this poverty-stricken land.

John, therefore, was the only personal servant to go on with me to Aïr—faithful, cheerful John, who did not care two straws where he went, so long as he had his master with him.

Therefore John and the camel-men were all that composed my following on the way to Agades, while the caravan was accompanied by the escort of six native soldiers, who had been detailed by the officer at Tanout to escort me as far as Aderbissinat, where there was a small Fort midway on my journey.

I intended to leave Takoukout on the night of the 30th, for the moon was full and opportune for night travel.

The day was employed proportioning loads and securely roping them, when sufficient rope had been found, for it is astonishing how such things disappear in the careless hands of natives during a month in camp, and on this occasion, when packages came to be made up, many ropes were short and others destroyed by white ants. As there was no longer village nor market-place where such native commodities could be purchased, there was no alternative but to insist that the camel-men search the bush for suitable tree-bark which could be plaited into rude cords; and this task kept the men fully employed all afternoon.

With the aid of the light of the moon and brightly blazing camp-fires, the camels were loaded up about 11 p.m., and we filed out of the old stockade, which had been *home* for almost a month, and made slowly off into the shadowy bush.

Night travel always holds for me an element of adventure, and it is not without livening and keenly alert senses that one advances into the unknown in the dark in the wake of some dusky leader who has none of the apprehension which the tendency to blindness produces in the stranger who is ignorant of the lie of the land ahead. Under such circumstances night travel also holds novelty, and, although one loses the opportunity to view the landscape as one passes along, there is a freshening of the senses that makes ample compensation: I am aware that it is cool, and that in consequence it is good to be out in those common hours of sleep; I observe the gaunt outline of the phantom-like camels that advance without sound of foot-fall; I see the shadows of low trees that ever change their shapes as we wend our course in and out among them over the gleaming moonlit ways of sand; I hear, sometimes, the low soft speech of the camel-man in consultation, followed, as a rule, by the caravan being halted and the discordant roar of a camel, which jars on the calm night stillness, while the men are righting a load; . . . afterwards silence is regained, and we are as a part of the brooding night, the camels padding along quite noiselessly in the sand, and there is naught that I can hear but the slight creaking of a load that rests uneasily on a pack-saddle, and the gritty scrape of the hard-skin sandals of a shuffling camel-man near me.

When the moon went down about 3 a.m., we camped for a few hours in the bush, off-loading the camels and lying down to rest on the bare ground without troubling to unpack blankets.

At daybreak, 6 a.m., the journey was resumed, and we camped at the well known as Tchingaraguen about noon, having travelled 25 miles since we broke camp.

On the following day we again travelled a long distance, camping by the light of the moon, about 9 p.m., at the well named Tadélaka, being then only about 10 miles short of the small outpost at Aderbissinat. Throughout the day the type of bush country continued the same, in aspect and insomuch that there was no visible sign that it is inhabited, though we are aware that there are a few Tuaregs, and their herds hidden in the inscrutable land somewhere.

A LONELY TUAREG CAMP IN THE BUSH.

SUNDOWN IN THE DESERT.

Next morning, 2nd April, we made the short journey to Aderbissinat and halted for the day.

What a strange place Aderbissinat is: the whole no larger than a small farm-dwelling enclosed within a square zareba, which might be the fence of a crofter's garden, while immediately outside are the wells and one or two temporary native shelters. About the wells are grouped some lean listless cattle and goats, and some tired donkeys and camels belonging to passing caravans. How well they fit the desolate scene! Listen to the plaintive lowing of the thirsty cattle, not the common cry of a domestic beast, but a wild strange sound peculiar to the land—a deep rumbling forced-out bellow that tails away with terrible insistency to a wail of want so clear and expressive in sound that even humans can easily comprehend that the animals are in dire distress. The simple unadorned scene, which is but a tiny speck of habitation in a boundless virgin space, lies in a hollow, so that approaching it either from the south or the north one is almost upon it before it is discovered.

If any of my fellow-men should ever doubt the constancy of the old-fashioned prestige of the white race in Africa, which goes to uphold peace in the wildest corners of the continent, I should like to direct their attention to such a place as this. Aderbissinat stands alone in one of the bleakest spots that could well be imagined, and isolated to such an extent that, if it happened to be attacked, it might easily be wiped out in a night and its nearest neighbour remain in ignorance of the fact for days— Tanout lies 75½ miles south, and Agades 93½ miles north, while both flanks are open to unlimited unguarded ranges. Yet all the force within this tiny Fort is one French officer and one sergeant, and a mere handful of native troops. Is it conceivable that it is such a force as this that intimidates the unreliable natives of the immediate neighbourhood to uphold peacefulness, or that keeps away the powerful bands of robbers from the north? I think not; rather is the cause to be found in native tradition of the prowess of the white race, and their far-reaching rule. It is not of an immediate act of rashness that the usual native fanatic is afraid, but of the inevitable consequences that they know would sweep in upon them once they had raised the white man's wrath. So that, in a broad sense, it is simply this tradition of great power that safeguards Aderbissinat, and other undermanned posts of the kind that are dreadfully remote yet not hopelessly beyond the reach of the long arm of justice; and therefore *Tradition* represents an unseen strength that is unrecorded on any roll, yet is reliable and useful as an army of men, impotent though it be except in significant influence.

Diminutive though it is, Aderbissinat Fort serves more than one purpose: it guards a precious store of water on the edge of the desert, which furnishes half the water-supply that is necessary for caravans to carry on the journey to Agades, for the intervening desert is waterless except for one well at Abellama; it serves as a blockhouse half way between Tanout and Agades, and therefore is protection to the highway; while it is also an important relay and checking station for the transport of the large supplies, chiefly grain, that are constantly going north to Agades to feed the considerable forces that are stationed there. Native escort, on foot, invariably accompanies those caravans of supplies, and the duty, burdened with rifle and accoutrements, is a very hard one in such a climate; so much so, that it is only by a series of relays that the escort for the total journey is successfully maintained. Thus, escort from Tanout is relieved at Aderbissinat, and fresh men take on the journey to Agades. Also, on occasions, the animals of a caravan are changed at Aderbissinat and others complete the journey.

Therefore, when all things are considered, Aderbissinat is of much importance to the transport of the country, and to the existence of Agades, and I am inclined to think that it has always held something of this importance as an outlying gateway to Aïr, for all Tuaregs, whether old or young, claim it to be within the southern boundary of their territory, though it is fully 100 miles from the foot of the Aïr mountains; and no doubt it is in consequence of their claim that the French authorities recognise it as within Aïr at the present time.

There are five caravan stages between Aderbissinat and Agades, known to the natives as Timboulaga, Tessalatin, Abellama, Tegguidi, and Tilaràderas. The camping-ground known as Timboulaga is within the bush-belt, but the others are all in the open desert, which commences about 19 miles north of Aderbissinat.

I continued my journey on the following day, leaving Aderbissinat in the cool of the late afternoon, and utilising the kindly moon to light us on our way until camping-ground was chosen, about midnight, some distance beyond Timboulaga.

On the next day, which was a Sunday (4th April), we again did not move until the afternoon, while the camels, fifteen of them, were turned out in the bush to partake of a good meal, as fodder promised to be less plentiful ahead. Under suitable conditions, camels should be allowed to graze at least five or six hours each day after halt is made.

Early in the day I shot two gazelles to augment the food supplies of the natives, and put in rather an uncomfortable time thereafter, for, when the sun rose high overhead, we were left without shade, and enjoyable rest was thereby impossible. In the full midday hours the sun is so directly overhead, that on no side of the dwarf, thin-leaved bush is there shade, which is a circumstance that reminds me to recount the wisdom of my camels, for, if the tired beasts happen to be off loaded about that time of day, they all proceed to select, with perfect knowledge and precision, the north-east side of the thickest bush available, thus choosing resting-places exactly where shade will be thrown later on when the sun commences to swing into the west.

I had intended to travel again at night, but the sun became so irksome, that I grew very restless, and about 2 p.m. was glad to call the camels in and start loading up, even though it entailed unpleasant labour for the camel-men in the intense heat.

Three hours after leaving Timboulaga we ascended

perceptibly to country of changed aspect, where the land was a desert of sand-dunes, and sand-pockets, and level pools of small gravel. This was the beginning of the desert, and the end of earth's fertility; behind lay the bush that struggled for a patchy existence in an ungenerous soil, which was a circumstance sad enough, yet infinitely more blessed did that barely clad beggary seem when compared with the awful desolate deadness of desert, which was, in general, unable to support life altogether.

On this night we camped at Tessalatin, which was but a name in a drear level land of sand. The altitude there was 1,875 ft., 225 ft. above Aderbissinat, which now lay 31 miles behind.

On the following day we left camp at 3.30 p.m. and camped at Abellama about 11 p.m. Throughout the journey we travelled over level desert— desert cloudless and pale as the sky, but of a buffish or khaki tone, and in places covered with tussocks of hardy grass, which catch and hold the loose sands that are the sweepings of the wind, so that they bank up in mounds and wave-crests, and bear the appearance of sand-dunes on the sea-shore. Here and there a tiny thorn bush, alone and hardly living; at other times, a scattered group of bushes that find existence possible and a little easier, since they are banded together, and each protecting the other from exposure to the onslaught of withering sand-storms. After crossing a gradual rise to a height of land about mid-journey to-day, we began a slight descent toward Abellama (alt., 1,700 ft.), where there is a deep well which is said to be as ancient as the old caravan roads across Africa, and which is the only place where water is to be found between Aderbissinat and Agades; so that, though drear and comfortless and lacking in everything that is picturesque, Abellama is a name that is conjured with by weary men of the caravans that travel there thirsting for water and sorely in need of replenishing the precious store that for some days has been slowly diminishing in sagging goat-skins.

At Abellama, as there was no shady bush to camp beside, I resorted to rigging up the baggage tarpaulin in the open desert, and camped under a few feet of shade like the veriest gipsy Tuareg.

As the months advance, so is the temperature increasing, and now that there was less protection than ever from the sun, it seemed to me that I was experiencing greater heat than I had ever known, and heat that was terribly exhausting.

The cause of the exceedingly fierce temperature (105° Fahr. to-day in the shade) may be accounted for in the fact that the sand is a ready medium for holding and reflecting the heat of the sun. As an example of this: if a man sit on a camel for some time, with feet dangling downwards, the sole-leather of boot or shoe or sandal, which is facing the sand and not the sun, becomes so heated that the feet are vastly uncomfortable, while if he should dismount and place weight upon them, the soles will be found to be so burning hot that he will exclaim with pain.

When evening came on this day, the caravan did not move off, as I had intended, for a change had come over me, and, for the first time, I felt too weak to go on. Dysentery and fever were upon me, illness which seemed to be the outcome of some kind of mild sunstroke, for I was quite dizzy and confused. The night's rest helped me little, and I spent the next day also in camp, feeling very miserable in my hot, improvised shelter. It was a bad place to be caught ill in—no restful shade at hand, not even scraggy bush, indeed, hardly enough wood to make a camp-fire; nothing but wastes of dreary sun-bleached desert.

One lay all day and almost panted in the heat, and thanked God with a deep sigh of relief when the sun went down.

At the end of the second day I felt I must make an effort to move on, and therefore called John and the camel-men to my couch upon the sand, and bade them prepare to start at midnight, even if it was found necessary to rope me to my camel so that I should not collapse and fall to the ground from weakness. This resolution was carried out, and about 1 a.m. the caravan was *en route* under the blessed coolness of the night, and aided by the light of the moon, which rose about the time the men commenced to load up the camels.

Tegguidi was reached not long after daylight, which enabled the caravan to negotiate the rough descent of the Pass in the cliff that is there without serious mishap to the loads, and we camped in due course on the flat plain that lay below. By which time I felt somewhat better, though I did not completely recover until some days later, when privileged to rest and shelter in a cool mud-house at Agades.

The abrupt change in elevation which occurs at Tegguidi is very remarkable and the cliff the most unique geological occurrence that I had thus far seen. It is a striking line of sheer cliff, which is very rugged in countenance, while at the base there are bankings and columns of detached rock and huge boulders. Advancing from the south, no sign of the cliff is visible until you arrive almost at the very edge of it, and look down over the grim countenance that faces the north, and out upon the pale sand-plains that stretch away from a level 200 ft. below. One is forcibly reminded of the open sea and rugged coast that stems the tide, for the whole formation, stretching east and west as far as eye can see, is like to the cliffs of the sea-shore, and one wonders in what age and by what force of elements it was fashioned to be so complete a barrier, and if it holds some strange geological secret.

Tegguidi cliff is of interest to sportsmen, for a few Barbary sheep are to be found there, while I received reliable reports of one or two lions seen in the vicinity (probably the rare nameless beast), which is quite feasible, as there is a tiny spring of water at a point known as Irhayen further east on the same cliff.

A comfortless day was put in at Tegguidi, trying to rest as best we could lying out on the bare plain as before, while the camels foraged for thriftless pickings.

With the advent of the moon we thankfully stole away from the place in the middle of the night.

When day broke, the caravan did not camp, for, anxious on account of my health and our small water store, I kept moving on until 2.30 p.m., when we camped about 11 miles from Agades, after having been thirteen hours on the march. Desert was crossed throughout the journey, dreary country of sand-dunes and great flat stretches of sand, with occasional gravel rises, which were sometimes buff like the sand and sometimes grey, but the pebbles always as level and neat as if set in place by the hands of skilful workmen. During the journey there was practically no change in elevation, which remained about 1,600 ft.

Again we snatched brief rest in the early part of the night and then travelled on to Agades, reaching our destination on the morning of the sixth day of travel (10th April), every man and beast of the caravan dreadfully tired; not because of the distance we had come, 93 miles, but on account of the ravaging sun, and for want of adequate sleep and proper food and water.

A note in my diary at this time reads: "It is uncanny land to travel through—barren of everything—dead like the ashes of a furnace fire—in no way beautiful, in nothing inspiring. . . . I was really glad when I entered Agades."

CHAPTER IX
AGADES

A GADES is not, as one might imagine from a glance at the map, close under the Aïr mountains, but is well out from them, and situated on the border of the desert. From Agades the low foothills of the mountains, not a continuous range, but individual elevations, with gaps between, are visible, blue in the distance, in the north, over some low acacia and evergreen "Abisgee" (Hausa) bush, which is growing, not far away, along a wide, very shallow river-bed that holds water but for a day or two during the surface rush of water that follows the rare torrential bursts of rain which sometimes occur in July or August.

It is a very great pleasure to sight those hills; to feast eyes that are weary of looking over limitless space upon this tangible promise of new and wonderful scene, already touched with the restfulness of the greys and browns of mountain slopes that cannot be altogether robbed of their richness by the blinding glare of overbold sunlight. Great is the contrast between mountain and desert, but greater still the change after the long, long journey through the featureless land to the south, for from the seaboard on the West Coast, from Lagos to Agades, there is no majestic range of like kind to those mountains of Aïr.

Agades is an ancient town; not large, not encircled by a great wall, not imposing, except for the high tapering tower of the old Mohammedan mosque which stands sentinel above everything in the land. It is, indeed, not much more than a cluster of clay-built tiny dwellings that crouch tenaciously upon the desert to exist as best they can amid driving winds and drifting sands that sweep over a landscape that is as open as the sea. Therefore, in truth, Agades to-day bears much of the woeful appearance of an outcast, and stands on a site of singular choice in surroundings over-barren to adequately support the inhabitants, who gain most of their livelihood far afield on the caravan routes.

Yet Dr. Barth, who passed through Aïr 70 years ago, wrote of Agades, with reference to its notable position in African history: "It is by the merest accident that this town has not attracted as much interest in Europe as her sister town Timbuktu."[7]

But the heyday of the greatness of Agades is past, though it is still a name of fame known to every native throughout the length and breadth of the western Sahara, which renown it has attained since it has long been a place of importance on one of the great caravan routes across Africa, and in olden times, as the chief town of Aïr, was a famous place where pilgrims journeying to and fro from Mecca halted and forgathered. Very, very old is Agades, and one cannot well conceive the changes that have taken place since its beginning, yet I am prone to think that the land, at least, was more fertile, less sand-enveloped than to-day, and offered less hardship to existence, for there is remarkable evidence of decline in the population of Aïr; a decline which has apparently been devolving very slowly, to judge by Dr. Barth's remarks concerning Agades in 1850—remarks which strangely enough could be applied with equal accuracy as it appears to-day. "The streets and the market-places were still empty when we went through them, which left upon me the impression of a deserted place of bygone times; for even in the most important and central quarter of the town most of the dwelling-houses were in ruins."[8] A concluding remark in my own diary of 1920 reads: ". . . but it is a sad place, belonging to an age of the Past; half-deserted, half-dead; full of the melancholy of the lone land which surrounds it." Though 70 years separate those two descriptions of the atmosphere of Agades, they are strangely alike in fact.

But to come down to recent times, Agades was occupied by the French in 1904 (16 years ago). In that year a military mission joined in with the great caravan of thousands of camels that once a year, at the time of the Rains when desert travel is possible, journey to the oasis of Fachi and Bilma, east of Aïr, to bring back to Hausaland a great store of salt obtained from salt-springs there. This mission left Zinder in August and reached Agades on 12th September, where it met with a friendly reception. In time a small pill-box of a fort was established about a mile north of the native town, which, by the way, was the one which withstood siege during the Rising of 1916, under the leadership of the northern rebel Kaossen, and Tegama, the traitor Sultan of Agades. Since then a large fort, many times the size of the original, has been erected about the old building, and equipped with modern weapons of war even to the inclusion of a wireless plant which receives daily news from Lyon, via Zinder.

Besides the Fort at Agades, there is also a strong camel corps maintained in the territory. On occasions this mobile force is camped at Agades, but more often it is forced to move from place to place along the borders of the desert, so that fodder may be found sufficient for the needs of the large number of camels.

Altogether the military force at Agades is a powerful one, which is due to the need that exists to combat and confound the constant depredations of armed robbers. Strange though it may seem in those modern times, Agades to-day is the centre of continual skirmishing activity, and Aïr the happy hunting-ground of daring bands of robbers, who descend upon it in search of such loot as camels, and goat herds, and young men and women to serve as slaves. Hogar and Tébu robbers are the most notorious and persistent miscreants to visit Aïr at the present time, but others from even greater distances are not unknown. For instance, last year (1919) the territory was visited by a band of the Requeibat tribe, said to be some 200 strong, from Cape Juby in the Spanish possessions of Morocco.

But later on I will deal more fully with the subject of robbers, which I have brought up here for a moment, since it has important bearing on the military composition of Agades.

The troops at Agades, or elsewhere in the Territoire Militaire, are chiefly Senegalese natives, while there is also a scouting force of camel-mounted goumiers, composed of local Tuaregs. Altogether there are eleven Europeans at Agades—French officers and N.C.O.s of the regular Colonial Service.

In the old town, apart from the Fort, there is a civic population of some 1,400 Tuaregs, and, in addition, some Hausa traders from the south, and an Arab or two from the north.

At the time of my visit food was remarkably scarce among the natives of Agades, and they were actually living from hand to mouth almost in a state of famine, though there was still three months to run before the Rains were due which promised new grain crops and new grazing for the herds. But, from all accounts, scant rations and poverty may be associated with Agades at most times, and far out on the caravan routes the traveller is warned that there is "nothing to eat at Agades," while the native soldiers, who get the best that is going under any circumstances, obviously dread being detailed for service there on account of its impoverished condition. On my way north, one of the senior officers at Zinder, speaking of the white men at Agades, remarked to me: "The climate, it is good; we have men there who are strong; but, oh! they are not fat.—Ah, no! they are not fat."

The fact of the matter is, Aïr, at the present time, is far from self-supporting in what she produces. This, in part, appears to be due to the barren nature of the country, and to lack of rains, but to a certain extent I believe it to be due to the indolent nature of the Tuareg inhabitants, who are essentially wandering fickle nomads, and not ardent toilers in the fields.

Of food-stuffs, Aïr produces goat herds which furnish the people with a certain amount of milk, cheese, and meat; some wild game which is snared for the flesh and hides; and a limited amount of dates, which are gathered during the Rains. Domestic poultry, which one associates with every native village in Africa, are here kept in very small numbers, as there is little grain for them; and it is often difficult to secure a single bird or a few eggs.

There are few villages in Aïr that can boast of inhabitants to-day, and only at three of those is there any grain grown, viz. at Azzal, Aouderas, and Timia, where small garden-plots on the river-bed banks, which are watered daily from wells, are cultivated to produce a small quantity of wheat and millet.

Yet grain is undoubtedly the chief food of the natives of Aïr, and, therefore, since they do not grow it, as much grain (millet, guinea-corn, and maize) as they can afford has yearly to be imported into Aïr on camel caravans and donkey caravans, which travel for this purpose to Tanout and Zinder, and even to Kano, 397 miles distant from Agades.

I was, unfortunately, only able to remain a few days at Agades before proceeding into the mountains, and, so far as the strange old town is concerned, I will not attempt to describe it fully, since I have not had sufficient opportunity to study the ancient history of the place—that all-important background which is the very soul of its significance, and which may only be comprehended after long examination, aided by the wisdom of the oldest inhabitants or learned Senussi, Marabout, or Mohammedan priests.

I have in mind, however, two notable dwellings in Agades with which I am familiar. The first I would like to describe is the Sultan's Palace, the most notable building in Agades excepting the imposing Mohammedan mosque, and, perhaps, of greater interest now than hitherto, since it was so lately the home of the traitor sultan Tegama, who at the time of my visit lay awaiting trial on the charge of high treason within the fort scarce a mile away. (Tegama, however, never stood trial, for he committed suicide about a month later.)

Through a deep archway in a thick mud wall you enter the courtyard of the Sultan's Palace. A small gloomy entrance, wherein one can well imagine lurked the watchmen of the Sultan in time of danger. On the outside of this entrance is a double-leaved, cumbersome door, constructed with palm poles laced securely together with thongs of goat-hide—a door to be closed at night to shut out the dangers of the desert. Do not picture a courtyard within the entrance that is paved and spotless for the reception of the footsteps of royalty or you will be disappointed, for there is nothing but an open space of level sand, with small mud buildings erected in such position that they form a fairly regular square. On the east is the palace; on the south the stall-divided mosque for private prayer; on the west an open shelter, presumably for the reception of travellers waiting audience with the Sultan or his advisers; and on the north the wall wherein the entrance. The palace is deserted—forsaken since the downfall of Tegama—and there is now no pleasant scene within the courtyard, so that one can but imagine those better days when camp-fires sparkled here at eventide surrounded by the hum of camp-fire gossip, and groups of picturesquely clad Tuaregs and reposing camels of wayfarers arrived with news or food from distant parts. Or the scene by day: the courtyard almost empty (as it is now), since the fierce heat of the sun had driven the people to seek shelter within the dark chambers of the palace, and the town, after the early hours of coolness, had witnessed the directing of the business of the day.

To enter the palace from the courtyard you turn to the left, and again you pass within a deep dark entrance. You are then in a gloomy windowless mud-built vestibule or entrance hall, with large fireplaces recessed at either end, while the room is crossed diagonally, to a door in the opposite wall, by a path that has raised margins. No doubt the convenient spaces on either side of the path were loitering places, where servants of the Sultan gossiped, the while they observed all who entered or passed out. Proceeding, one steps from the vestibule through the door in the opposite wall, and is again outdoors in the full daylight (which is most noticeable after the darkness of the den-like interior), having entered a small inner courtyard hemmed in by dwellings on all sides and containing a confusing number of low dark doorways and ascending stairways to dwellings above. Directly opposite the vestibule is the low door which gives entrance to the throne-room, a diminutive chamber with arched ceiling beams, which contains the throne dais, fashioned, like all structure, with the clay-soil from neighbouring pits, and rounded off plainly, but not without some neatness and endeavour at rude design. As to the rest of the chamber, there are a few small niches in the thick walls, and some interesting quaintly primitive scroll ornament, while on the right of the throne there is an exposed mud-built stairway leading up to a second story, wherein are three low-ceilinged rooms lit by small openings in the exterior wall, each room a tiny gloomy shut-in space more like hiding-den or prison than chosen human dwelling. The doors from the inner courtyard lead to many other such apartments, no less diminutive, no less gloomy, and now but the home of swarms of bats and one or two large brown African owls (*Bubo africanus cinerasceus*). Throughout one finds the same congestion of space, the same rude adaptability to the bare needs of shelter of primitive outdoor people, which is common to every native dwelling in Hausaland or Aïr, or, indeed, anywhere in out-of-the-way places in Africa. The entire dwelling, and many another of the kind in similar country, is a "Palace" only in name and political significance. And this condition of primitiveness and humbleness ought, I think, to be made quite clear, for I have read works which, in my view, were far too apt to lead one astray in forming an overhigh opinion of the royalty and magnificence which is sometimes believed to surround the Emir or Sultan or Saraki of a native community and their dwellings. True, such men are the kings and princes of the land, and have a certain exalted standing; but there is a very wide difference between those chiefs of tribes or districts (who are sometimes not much more than crafty rascals, and seldom to any notable degree better in refinement than their subjects) and the kings of civilised lands. And the great difference in caste between primitive King and cultured King is in no way more clearly reflected than through the medium of their dwellings and environments: in the one case a beautiful palace, rich in architecture, refined, and royally appointed in every inner detail; in the other nothing more important than a group of small bare mud-built dwellings, neither tastefully appointed nor regal in any degree, and entirely wrapped in an atmosphere of humbleness, even poverty, such as surrounds all people of primitive environment and primitive race.

Mosque.
VIEW OF AGADES.

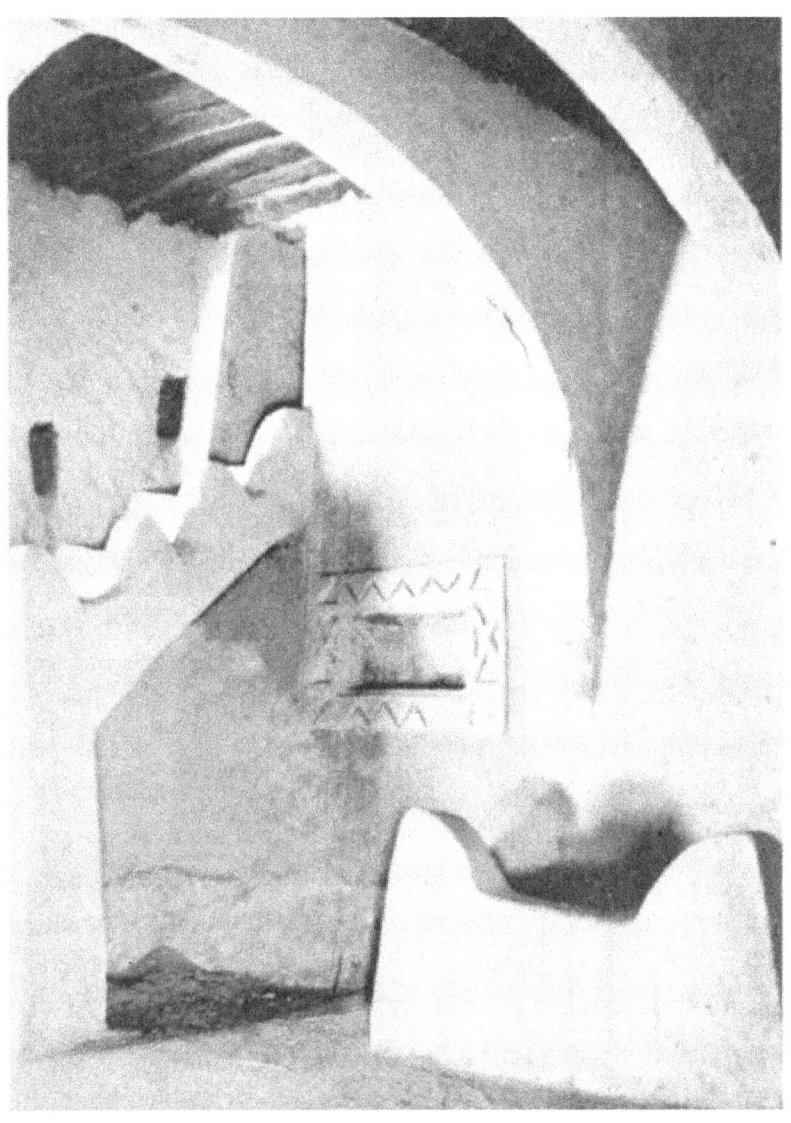

THRONE-ROOM OF THE SULTAN OF AGADES.

The position of the Sultan of Agades is one of greatness in the land, though of a type of local importance which has decided limitations, and one might be forgiven, if, carried away by the weight of rank and reputation, he should expect to find about the Sultan's abode something in keeping with the name of a sovereign. But that is not so, for we find the throne-room a small dark space, within earthen walls, no larger than a cottage bedroom, and less ornamented; and his private apartments for his own use, and the use of his retinue, no larger, no more attractively or extravagantly constructed, than tiny cellars or pen-like outhouses.

So that the Sultan's Palace at Agades, like many others in Africa, is a humble place indeed, its virtue not at all in regal magnificence, but in historic value, and in the novelty and quaintness of primitive native architecture of a character of great simplicity and antiquity as if it has remained unchanged through time by any process of civilisation.

The second dwelling I will describe is not in the old town of Agades, nor is it of native design. I write of the European mess-room within the Fort, part of a dwelling of European conception, built with some knowledge of design, and imposing and spacious in comparison with the diminutive buildings of the native town, but, nevertheless, a dwelling rude enough in construction, since, by nature of its wilderness environment, it is, in essentials, impossible to avoid the limitations imposed by primitive labour and primitive material.

I will give the description, such as it is, informally from my diary, since it embraces a little of the life, as well as the architecture, common to the white man at the Fort of Agades:

"We had forgathered for breakfast, that customary eleven o'clock meal of the French which is both breakfast and lunch in one, at that time of day when it is an ordeal merely to cross the barrack square, so white and glaring the sand, so great the fierceness of the sun. Therefore, one by one, the labours of the morning over, we stepped into the shade and coolness of the thick walled room with a real thankfulness; especially thankful, perhaps, those who bear the mark of chronic fatigue, which an unnatural climate is so apt to impose, and which is apparent upon the features of most of the group. Around small tables that were pushed together to make up one large one we sat down to the meal, the company being composed of five French officers and myself, while our dusky native servants were in attendance, and a small child stood to one side and pulled the cord that swung a punka which was suspended over the table.

"We sat long over the repast, discussing many things African, and it was not until some time after the meal was over that conversation lagged at my end of the table and gave me an opportunity to observe my surroundings. The room is not very large, and there is just space enough to allow the attendants to pass comfortably around the table. Trimless, square-cut liberal openings serve as doors and windows, while over those are dropped blinds of light lattice, which prevent the entrance of sun and sand-dust, yet admit a free current of air. The mud walls are thick and straightly built, smoothed down with a coating of mud plaster, and whitewashed with a preparation of chalk and cement, obtained out of the ground in the neighbourhood. (Dr. Barth in his works makes reference to a house nicely whitewashed in the old town of Agades, but he did not mention the interesting fact that the "whitewash" is native to Agades.) The walls are bare of ornament except for cupboards, set back against them, that are made from an assortment of packing-cases and still retain their true character, even to the glaring names of merchant and merchandise in their rude transformation and paintlessness. But what better can be done where sawn boarding is unknown?

The ceiling of the room is lofty, and constructed with closely set undressed fibrous dum palm timbers, the only wood in the country that the terrible white ant will not destroy. Upon the walls, in the darkest places, there are a number of wart-like lumps which are the plaster-built cell-nests of black-and-yellow hornets that pass constantly in and out of the room. Also there are one or two pairs of tiny waxbills at freedom in the room, cheeping and flitting from floor to window-ledge, or vanishing outdoors. They are always in pairs, inseparable as love-birds, the male crimson in colour and his mate mouse-brown. I must call them *Estrilda senegala bruuneiceps*, so that there may be no error on account of their scientific identity, but to ordinary folk, such as you and me, I would describe them as 'Crimson Waxbill' or 'House Waxbill.'

"I think I have described all, when eyes roam nearer hand and dwell on the few articles on the table, and I see that even there we do not escape the primitive: the pepper is in a cigarette tin which still bears the *yellow* label of the manufacturer; the salt is in another distinguished by a *green* label; while all the drinking-glasses are dark-coloured and thick and ragged-rimmed, and are nothing more than old wine bottles cut down about their centre."

And from all this we may perhaps justly conclude that the Sultan's Palace is about the best the natives can do in the way of dwelling-building at Agades, and the mess-room at the Fort a fair sample of the humble extent that civilised people can improve upon it when thrown entirely on the scant resources of a wilderness.

CHAPTER X
AÏR: NORTH TO BAGUEZAN MOUNTAINS AND HUNTING BARBARY SHEEP

O^N 26th April I left Agades with the intention of travelling north into the Aïr mountains, and to ultimately pitch a base camp on Baguezan.

Besides four transport camels, the little band which set out was made up of two goumiers, by name Saidi and Atagoom, the chief of Baguezan, and two followers and myself; six fully armed camel-mounted men, not including my cook-boy, John, who was also in the company. The Chief of Baguezan had been called into Agades so that, if he was friendly disposed, he could conduct me to his country. He was the new Chief Minerou who had succeeded Yofa, who was foully killed a few months before by the dagger-thrust of a skulking foe when guarding his camels against an attack from prowling robbers.

At Agades, before departure, I had stored every article I could do without, on account of the difficulties of travel ahead, and took with me supplies of food and ammunition barely sufficient to last for a period of two or three months.

Our little band left Agades at various times in the afternoon to camp at the tent-like inhabited Tuareg village of Azzal, which was only about five miles N.E. of our starting-point, and was to be the rendezvous of our organised departure on the morrow.

27th April.—Left Azzal before dawn. Yesterday we had skirted the foothills in travelling up the broad dry river-bed of the shallow Azzal Valley, but to-day we departed from the edge of the level desert, and entered low hill country of strange appearance, composed of rock and boulder and gravel, bare of any vegetation, and therefore dreadfully melancholy and barren. View after view of brown coloured hills unfolded before us as we passed onward over gravel-strewn ground, or picked our way through rocky outcrops, or descended to sandy river-bed; while always one could follow out the thin line of the river banks or hollows which caught moisture in the rains, for they contained a bright green growth of dum palm and "abisgee"[9] bush, which was very striking and conspicuous among the sombre hills.

Without any doubt it is beyond Azzal that the traveller enters the true brown-grey rock country of Aïr: the low country, which contains many isolated cone-shaped hills or kopjes, that leads one, in time, to the great central mountains. Bare the land is of generous elements of beauty, and almost equally bare of living thing. In many places the only vegetation in a large area lies in the thin rift of some infant rivulet—a meandering line of sand which seeks a way among the grey pebbles and rocks, wherein a few dry tufts of grass, and, perhaps, a stunted dwarf acacia, a grasshopper or two, and, if you are in luck, a small mouse-like, sand-coloured lark crouching on the ground may be seen, for scarcely any moving living thing misses the eye in a land that is well-nigh motionless.

We camped at Solom Solom about noon, and obtained some water from a well which is on the banks of a river there, and about which one or two Tuaregs are camped. The Tuaregs with me pronounce this name Selim Selim. It is about 18 miles due north of Azzal, and has altitude of 2,100 ft. (Agades is 1,710 ft.)

28th April.—Left Solom Solom an hour before daybreak; reached Tchefira about noon, after stopping to replenish our water-skins in the river-bed known to the natives as Arrajubjub. Water obtained by digging down in the sand of the river-bed close under some large rocks on the east bank of the stream.

There is a height of land at Arrajubjub where the river falls south to Agades and north toward Baguezan. The river valley, which we chiefly followed to-day, and which turns almost due east not long after leaving Solom Solom, is named in sections, as are most rivers in the country: thus it is the Solom Solom (which becomes the Azzal river further south) at the beginning of to-day's journey, then Dabaga, then Injerwdan, then Arrajubjub, and, finally, Tchefira. The river banks continue to have the green fringe of vegetation: dum palms, Hausa *Kaba*; small skunk-smelling tree, Hausa *Abisgee*; small dwarf acacia, growing 3 ft. to 4 ft. high, Hausa *Giga*; and a fairly large acacia, say, 20 ft. high, Hausa *Zandidi*.

MY CARAVAN ON THE ARRAJUBJUB RIVER.

TYPICAL AÏR LANDSCAPE.

Some picturesque hill country was passed through, though the hills remain bare of vegetation. The large mountain range of Aouderas was sighted faintly in the north about 11 a.m., distant a little more than 20 miles.

A number of Dorcas Gazelles were seen at Tchefira and a single Dama Gazelle.

29th April.—To-day our direction of travel changed to about due N.E., while we kept chiefly in touch with the Araouat River, sometimes travelling up its heavy sandy bed, sometimes branching off to make a short cut overland when the river took a large circuitous bend. The hills we passed to-day in the stony uneven plains were mostly conical and of blackish lava rock or reddish dust. About 6 miles from Tchefira there is a prominent hill which the Tuaregs call Nafurifanya, and below this hill, on the west side, we found a single native working on a section of ground that contained a salt deposit, which mineral he collected by digging one foot to three feet below the sand surface. At the end of our journey, after travelling a considerable distance over gravel-covered country, we intersected a narrow river-bed, named Arra (not on map), where we camped for the day, in view of Baguezan, lying north, and Aouderas, north-west: both very large mountains, of which Aouderas appears the lesser in extent but the greater in height. Many of the lower hills between Baguezan and Aouderas are of striking shapes; two noteworthy with tower-like peaks, and the others strangely cone-shaped.

Altitude at camp, 3,000 ft.

30th April.—Travelled onward in the early morning, and camped two to three miles north-west of Teouar (a deserted village of stone-built huts), close in under Baguezan foothills, at a place selected by Minerou as a suitable camping-ground from which to hunt among the hills for mountain sheep. We were still in the district known to the natives as Arra, so named apparently on account of the river course that has its source in the mountain of that name, which is the most northern of a group of three prominent elevations that lie immediately to the west of this camp, named respectively, from south to north, Tchebishrie, Aouderas, and Arra.

When camp was selected, brackish water was obtained from the Arra river by digging in the sandy bottom, but there was no rich vegetation on the banks.

Thus far, north of Agades, good water had been found at Azzal and Solom Solom in wells, and at Arrajubjub by excavation. No water was drawn at Tchefira, except for the camels, as it was brine-tasted and not good, and there was no water at our first camp on the Arra river on 29th April.

Altitude at camp, 3,300 ft.

About 3 p.m. I set out with Minerou to tramp to the mountains to search for sheep, and had my first experience of the nature of the hunting that lay before me in looking for those animals. The ruggedness of the country was astonishing. To begin with, the apparently flat stony land that lay between camp and the hills was, on closer acquaintance, found to be thickly seared with deep ravines, and although Minerou, who knew the country like a book, led me by the easiest route, our path was constantly barred by those strange deep channels, down which we scrambled, over rocks and stones, to afterwards ascend with no little effort to the opposite side. The nearer we drew to the hills, the rougher became the nature of the country, and our outward journey culminated at the base of Arra in one long scramble among huge boulders and loose stones, where foothold had to be picked out at each step as we hurried on, for Minerou, born mountaineer and barefooted (for he had removed his sandals the better to grip foothold as he stepped or jumped from rock to rock), was covering the ground at a great pace. We had planned, in setting out, that we would not have sufficient daylight to climb the mountain, and would skirt a part of the base in the hope that at dusk we might chance upon sheep descending from the mountain tops (where they remain all day) to feed on the sparse vegetation in the ravines. However, our search went unrewarded, although I had the pleasure of actually seeing one animal perched away up on the mountain-side at a great height.

During the outing I saw some birds of great interest, and I particularly made note of three species which I had not observed further south, and which, later, proved to be the Rock Pigeon (*Columba livia targia*), the beautiful Sandgrouse (*Pterocles lichtensteinii targins*), and a small sombre wheatear-like bird (*Ceromela melanura airensis*) of blackish-brown colour of striking similarity to the rocks and stones on which they perch.

1st May.—Away before daylight to hunt in earnest for wild sheep. To-day we did not go to the mountains lying N.W., but made for some lower more isolated hills in the north, the principal one of which the Tuaregs call Tuckazanza. The chief of Baguezan and one of his men accompanied me. Travelling was as hard as that experienced yesterday, over rough mountain sides and valleys of rocks and boulders and stones, while in some cases whole hills were composed of huge boulders, individually many tons in weight, which could only be negotiated by reckless bounding and leaping and scrambling, while deep ugly chasms held open mouth to receive you should you slip. I have hunted in many strange places, but never in such wild mountainous country as this; I feel I cannot compare it with anything at home: the nearest to it in ruggedness that I know is where one may hunt for sea otters along the cliff-shores of the storm-torn coasts of the Orkney Islands.

About 7.30 a.m., having seen no sheep, we held a consultation, when Minerou decided that he would climb right over the summit of Tuckazanza, while his follower and myself were directed to go further round the base and climb over a lower spur, and we were eventually to meet again on the other side. This arranged, we started off on our separate ways. In due time I, along with Minerou's follower, had climbed to the summit of the ridge, always scanning every fresh hollow or rise as they appeared in view in hope of sighting game; but thus far without any luck.

We had begun the descent down the other side, when the native beside me suddenly gripped my arm and pointed excitedly to the right, where, after a few moments of perplexity in endeavouring to locate that which the Tuareg had seen, my eyes were arrested by the slight movement of a pair of heavy curved horns. Not a hair of the animal was in sight, but the head undoubtedly belonged to a sheep standing not more than five hundred yards away in a slight dip in the mountain side. No time was to be lost: the horns were facing our way, and perhaps, for all we could tell, the wary animal had heard us and was looking upward, listening. I signed to the native to lead on, judging he would choose the easiest way through the huge boulders that we were among (I found in later experience that mountain sheep always frequent the very roughest places, where they the more readily find the coolest and darkest shelter from the heat and sunlight in the caves and chasms which gigantic boulders and rocks so readily form), and, crouching and scrambling and leaping, we set off on the stalk at a perilous speed—perilous at least to me, who could not boast the barefooted nimbleness of my mountaineer companion.

It was surely the "daftest" and the least cunning stalk I have ever made, excepting perhaps the "buck-fever" pranks of my earliest experiences of hunting. The native had simply grasped the idea that the animals looked like shifting when we sighted them, for he had seen two, and his one purpose was to get there before they could possibly be gone—and I had but to follow; for moments were precious, and what use to hesitate and stop to explain that I should advance slowly so that my footwear would make no scraping noise on the rocks, and slowly, also, so that I should have some breath and life in my body when the moment came to shoot. How I managed to cover the distance in our mad haste without mishap I do not to this day know, except that for the moment I had no time to think of fear, which certainly helped me on over ugly chasms that yawned across my path, entailing leaps that seemed beyond my ability, yet, somehow, were miraculously crossed and left behind.

We reached the place where the animal had stood, and, on peering over the slight rise which had screened us, at once saw two sheep clambering away over the rocks. I fired at once at the largest one and brought him down, but twice missed the second one as he headed away upwards, sometimes in view, more often hidden among the rocks.

However, as luck had it, we learned a little later, when Minerou joined us, that this second animal had run into him on the summit, and he had shot it, so that both animals were bagged.

Consultation decided that the follower and I should go back to camp for a camel to fetch in the game, while Minerou would return to his kill on the summit and safeguard it against jackals and crows (the latter were already croaking and cawing on the rocks about us, having detected the kills from afar with their extraordinary eyesight), as we had already secured ours, after disembowelling it, by moving it into a hollow between two rocks, and heaping upon it big stones so that nothing could reach the carcass.

On the way back to camp there occurred a strange incident that proved highly exciting for a moment, until the voices of friends banished the possibility of human bloodshed; an incident which demonstrated to me at an early stage how real is bandit warfare in those hills. This is what happened. We were about to cross a deep ravine, when we suddenly espied two men travelling toward us on foot, not on the open ground of the level land above, but perched up on the cliff face of the sunken ravine and advancing amongst the rocks, as if they had some purpose in remaining concealed. Instantly the native with me crouched behind cover and looked to the full charging of his rifle, quite apparently apprehending danger. In a few moments the men advanced around a spur and disappeared into a recess in the twisting ravine. Whenever they were out of sight my follower bounded forward, agile as a goat, among the huge rocks, to a prominence where he might carefully look over and down upon the approaching men and observe them more closely from a point of advantage, while I lay with my rifle ready and waited. But the native did not beckon me forward, or return himself, and soon I heard voices ring out, and knew we were with friends and not enemies, and a few moments proved them to be one of our own party, who had been sent away the night before by the Chief to scout through the neighbourhood as a precaution against robbers, and with him was a native from Baguezan whom he had chanced to meet.

The alarm had turned out to be false. Nevertheless, I did not readily forget my native's instant expectation of a fight with enemies, and the familiar manner in which he accepted the situation. His were the actions of one who lived from day to day in the midst of dangers, and had been bred and born to the habit of defence against foes that ever lurked near.

Many incidents of this character I experienced later on, and had soon learned that the alarming rumours relating to robbers which were prevalent farther south were all too true, and that the shadows of lurking foes were foremost in the thoughts of every Tuareg in Aïr, where robbers imposed a terrifying oppression.

On reaching camp, a camel was despatched to find Minerou in the hills and bring in the sheep, which in due course arrived in camp to be skinned and used as food, as neither beast was perfect enough to serve as a museum specimen. The larger of the two had a fine head, but the body hair was thin and patchy, and altogether out of condition.

A peculiar change in the hot cloudless weather had occurred during the past two days. Yesterday, in the afternoon, there was high wind and some rain showers, while to-day, at the same hour, the sky was overclouded, and distant thunder rumbled, and there was again very high wind which wrecked my tarpaulin shade-shelter and rudely interrupted the bird-skinning on which I was employed at the time. Possibly Rains are now falling in Nigeria, where, I am told by the natives, they are about due. But Rains are not due in Aïr until July or August, if local information is to be trusted.

2nd May.—Away again at peep of daylight, but to-day had no luck. The Chief and I followed the trail of a very large animal where it had been this morning feeding along the foot of the mountain named Ebodina, and when we had traced it over rocks and sand-pools in the ravines to where it had taken to the heights, we too started to ascend in hope of finding its resting-place in some cave above. And upward we laboured during the remainder of the morning, the sure-footed Chief sound of lung and never daunted, and I, bound to follow over the wildest mountain face imaginable, composed, like the hills we had hunted yesterday, chiefly of pile upon pile of huge boulders, with deep dark chasms between. Into the deepest of those recesses the Chief would sometimes pause to throw a pebble in the hope that it might send the sheep from its place of hiding in its noisy course as it bounded and trickled down into the gloomy well-like depth. But all to no avail, and we returned to camp empty-handed.

On this day I found the relics of a tragedy among the boulders near the foot of Ebodina. They were the rags of clothing and a few minute pieces of personal belongings, and a riddled goat-skin water-bag belonging to some native who had died there alone, either through falling from the rocks or from want of water or food. No weather-bleached bones lay beside those pitiful remnants, and without doubt jackals had long ago seen to their removal.

3rd May.—Similar to the previous days here, the weather dulled down in the afternoon, and we had high wind and thunder and a little rain, the wind being a great hindrance to skinning in my temporary quarters, for I have not built a grass-hut workshop here, as the ground is bad to excavate for post sockets—rocks and gravel— and wood and grass is very scarce.

No hunting except for small specimens, and none of the men left camp, save to keep watch over the camels, who have constantly a guard in case robbers should discover them.

The Chief of Baguezan is impatient to move on to the security of his mountain home, one long day's journey distant, but I ask him to have patience for a little, for here we are on low ground, and can hunt for bird and beast and butterfly which I may not find on the mountain-top of Baguezan.

4th May.—Dawn found Minerou and myself again among the deep ravines and rugged mountains in quest of sheep. Four animals were seen late in morning far up the mountain side of Aouderas, but we were unable to get near them. Signs of sheep are plentiful enough, but, so far as I can judge at present, they are very wary and wild and secretive in their movements, resting and hiding in the dark mountain caves by day, and coming out to feed in late evening and through the night.

Yesterday evening and to-day Rains have fallen quite heavily, and the hitherto dry river-bed at camp is to-day a shallow stream of water, which is a sight to gladden men's hearts in this land of terrible drought. The water in the river is very reddish on account of the soil of that colour which has been washed down from the ravine sides and mountain sides. Streams of water are also apparent to-day in ravines on the slopes of Baguezan Mountains, so that precious rain has fallen there also, and the Chief is now more anxious than ever to get back to his home.

I discussed the boundaries of Aïr with the Chief of Baguezan to-day. He states that Aderbissinat is within the boundary of Aïr, and that east and west their country terminates at the edge of the desert. He declares he knows nothing of the limits of Aïr to the north, and that his people never go there. "It is bad country, they are afraid to go," he said; while at the same time he informed me that none of his people would accompany me to Assodé or Iferouan when I declared my intention to visit those places. Moreover, he warned me solemnly that I would be very rash if I did not give up my intention of going farther into the country—a view expressed by every Tuareg native of Aïr with whom I discussed the subject previous to setting out north. From which it may be gathered that northern Aïr is indeed a place of evil repute.

To-day I trapped a beautiful silver-grey fox of a kind I had not seen before, which, I fancy, is peculiar to mountain country and not to be found in the desert. (Scientific examination has since proved it to be a new sub-species: *Vulpes rüppelli cæesia*.)

5th May.—Travelled far this day over most rugged country, but once again did not succeed in bagging sheep.

On returning to camp in the afternoon, blustering wind-squalls again made the skinning of small specimens almost impossible, and I suddenly made up my mind to pack up and go on to Baguezan, prompted partly by the unsatisfactory conditions at camp and partly by the wishes of the Chief and his men, who were impatient to reach their homes.

Thus closed the first few days of hunting in the Aïr mountains without any great measure of success. But I had thoroughly enjoyed the search for sheep amongst the wild grandeur of strange mountains and had found a type of hard hunting which, I fancy, would rejoice the heart of any sportsman. Moreover, in the Chief of Baguezan I had found a splendid hunter, full of shrewd knowledge of the habits of the animals of his country, a born mountaineer, active as a cat among the rocks, familiar with every nook and cranny in the hills, and tireless in his quest for game.

At a later date I was very successful in similar hunting, and secured fine representative specimens of the Barbary sheep of Aïr, which the Hausa natives name *Ragondoutchie* (or Ragonduchi) and the Tuaregs *Afitell*, and which has proved to be a new sub-species which Lord Rothschild has named *Ammotragus lervia angusi*.

The head of the best male specimen had horns measuring 21 ins. in length and of 20½ ins. span, while the animal weighed 152 lbs. The largest sheep I shot was an old one which weighed 164 lbs., with damaged horns that had no larger dimensions than those recorded above.

CHAPTER XI
IN BAGUEZAN MOUNTAINS

I HAD no sooner departed outside the immediate neighbourhood of the Fort of Agades, in commencing the journey to Baguezan, as described in the preceding chapter, than the Chief, Minerou, and his glib-tongued companions, who had all put their heads together-even the two goumiers joining in—endeavoured to dissuade me from my purpose to climb into Baguezan Mountains, and strongly advised my return to Agades. Their chief argument was that the camels carrying my stores could not possibly ascend the mountain pass. From which I judged that they were foolishly suspicious of the stranger, and did not want me to pry into their mountain stronghold. They kept up plying me with similar doubtful stories for the next three days, by which time we had camped at Arra, whereafter they desisted, seeing that I would on no account be shaken in my purpose before I had actually seen the pass in Baguezan. The following days of sheep hunting with the Chief brought us more closely together and enabled me to break down, at least outwardly, the barrier of distrust of me; until, in a moment of confidence, seeing that I would not be hoodwinked, he went so far as to admit that the ascent into Baguezan, for me and my stores, could be accomplished.

So that it transpired that on 6th May we climbed the slopes of Baguezan and entered the strange, awesome mountain stronghold.

There are, the natives declare, but two ways by which camels can enter Baguezan mountains: one in the southern slopes above a camping-place known to the natives as Tokede, which is the principal pass and that which we used, while the other (the only other pass I have seen, which endorses, to some extent, native statements) lies N.W., and is a means of exit to, or entrance from, the north, which is principally used at the present time by natives passing between Baguezan and Timia. Both are rocky, awkward paths, no wider than game-tracks, that wend their way zigzagging upward over steep slopes where foothold for beasts of burden has been searched for and found possible, while in many rough places the path has been hewn and excavated by the hands of men where it has been necessary.

Slowly the surefooted patient mountain-reared camels of Aïr succeed in ascending or descending these paths, sometimes slipping and falling to their knees, so treacherous the foothold, and always some beasts of the caravan make the journey at the expense of torn nails and bleeding feet.

When we had climbed half-way up Baguezan and had paused on a short levelled stretch to rest the distressed camels and their rock-bruised feet, as was necessary from time to time, I turned back and looked below, and out before me to the very horizon, on scenes the like of which in colouring and utter strangeness I had never witnessed before: to the west lay the mountains Tchebishrie, Aouderas, and Arra, and a score of others that are unnamed, all dark and towering and majestic; while in the forefront the rough lowland over which we had travelled now looked, from a height, like level flats, barren and blackish (on account of the porous lava rock and hard round pebbles which cover the land), as if they had been swept by fire and only the ash remained. The scenes are overflowing with a strange drear greyness, that fills the heart of man with sadness, except where deep ravines run out from the mountains and draw therefrom thin lines that have sometimes their beginning in the brightness of dum palms, or "Abisgee" bushes, which grow on dry river-banks of certain fertility, and which trend to lines of sand colour and the dull greyness of leafless acacias as they die away in the far distance of the lowland.

In four hours we had ascended to the summit, and were upon a plateau covered with innumerable rocky hills, through which we wandered in and out where passage for the camels was possible, and two hours later reached the small village of Tasessat, hidden in the hills, where I decided to pitch a permanent collecting-camp.

Baguezan mountains might be said to be two storeys high, the great plateau being the line of the first and principal level, whence arise countless hills with summits of various elevations. The altitude of Tasessat village, which is on the plateau, is 5,200 ft., about 2,000 ft. above the land at the mountain base of Baguezan, while a hill named Tarusszgreet, which is the highest rising from the plateau, has an altitude of 6,050 ft.

The plateau of Baguezan is perplexing to describe adequately. There are countless ranges of hills, sometimes with narrow sand-flats and river-beds between; massive hills formed of giant grey granite boulders, and others not nearly so numerous—with rounded summits and a surface of apparent overlappings and down-pourings of smooth loose reddish and grey fragments, as if the peaks were of volcanic origin, though no craters are there. But it is the formation of the many hills of giant granite boulders that make the scenes so astonishing, so rugged, and so unique—you might be on the roughest sea coast in the world, and not find scenes to surpass those here in desolation and wildness. They are hills that appear to the eye as if a mighty energy underneath had at some time heaved and shouldered boulder upon boulder of colossal proportion into position, until huge, wide-based, solid masses were raised upon the plateau. On the other hand there are instances where hills appear as if the forces underneath had built their edifice badly, and in a manner not fit to withstand the ravages of time, and those are places where part of the pile has apparently collapsed, and there remains a bleak cliff face and the ruins of rocks at the foot. Between the hills the narrow defiles which make up the plateau level are, in general, small places of sand, where scattered acacias grow (some to a fair height), and where, in certain places, dry shallow sandy stream-beds find a course: also there are flats, with ground surface of pebbles, which are bare as the hills that invest them.

From the plateau, or even from the lower hills, it is impossible to obtain a fair conception of the area of Baguezan mountains, since an extensive view is blocked in all directions by the hills which surround one on all sides. But from the top of Tarusszgreet a splendid view may be obtained. The great hill-bearing plateau is about 25 miles in diameter, with an edge that, viewed from the commanding height of Tarusszgreet, appears almost as round as a tea-cup. Looking down on the land on all sides from this pinnacle that permits an unbroken view north, south, east, and west, the scene is a memorable and a striking one: rocks, boulders, and grave greyness predominate all else, for, as far as an eye can see within the limits of Baguezan, nearly the whole land is one of barren hills—barren, that is, of fertility, but not of wild native beauty, even impressiveness. It strikes one most forcibly as a place of fearful poverty, but, even though the blackness of the grey rocks so strongly predominates, there are, as in the country south of Baguezan, brighter scenes on a miniature scale in the pleasant little basins or sandy pockets on the plateau, where, in places, the line of a dry stream-bed may be traced, and where straggling acacias stand darkly dotted against a buffish sandy background. Be the eye attracted to the broad masses of grey hills, or to the little gleams of golden sand, the view from the lofty height of Tarusszgreet, somewhat vaguely sad though it be, captures the appreciation of the mountaineer, who cannot help, unless he be an unresponsive soul indeed, being enraptured with the wonderful space of earth and sky which his position for the moment commands, and with the details of a hundred mysterious scenes contained within the miniature kingdom that lies beneath his feet. Particularly at sunrise or sunset is the view fair, when short-lived lights rest on the broad rugged surface of mountain-side scene, and dip delicately into the valleys to be absorbed by lurking shadows. Those are precious moments in a day, or, might I say, in a lifetime?

TYPICAL BOULDER COMPOSITION OF MANY
AÏR MOUNTAINS AND HILLS.

MINEROU, CHIEF OF BAGUEZAN, AND SAIDI, MY GOUMIER.

There is much beauty in Africa, though that is a circumstance which, I believe, we do not often realise or speak about, because, I fear, beauty is often missed, or at least fails to receive full appreciation, since, to view any fair picture with full and generous reflection, the individual or audience should be in the cleanness of health and good spirits that lead to enthusiasm and energy and praise; and, alas, such a state of mind is all too seldom the white man's lot beneath a sun that is hourly tapping his precious store of vitality.

In ascending to the plateau of Baguezan, one enters a secretive stronghold of a small band of Tuaregs, and I think it is because Baguezan is a natural fortification, for the most part inaccessible to robbers or to any stranger, that we to-day find any natives living in Aïr north of Agades and its immediate neighbourhood. I have said elsewhere that Timia, Aouderas, and Baguezan are the only places now inhabited in Aïr north of Agades, and both Timia and Aouderas are near to the foot of Baguezan, so that, when robbers threaten, the camels of the inhabitants of those two places can, if the danger warrants, be driven on to the plateau for safety, while the natives scatter broadcast among the rocks—a procedure which occurred once while I was there.

There are in Baguezan mountains at the present time six tiny villages. They are: Tasessat, the chief village where I camped, whence radiate the bearings given below; Argargar, about 8 miles distant from Tasessat, on a bearing of 330°; Ouwari, on the same bearing, not far from Tasessat, on the track to Argargar; Egulubilub, 3 to 4 miles from Tasessat, on a bearing of 140°; Emuludi, on the same bearing, about one mile distant from Tasessat; Atkaki, near Tasessat, on a bearing of 220°. Excepting Tasessat, none of these villages are on any map I possess.

The dwellings now in use in the villages are mere tiny, gipsy-like sun-shelters of a type common to the inhabitants of Aïr. They are constructed with lathes of wood bent over to form a dome framework, which is round in plan and a half-round in elevation. Upon the framework hay-grass is laced securely, or skins, to keep out sun and a certain amount of sand-dust. They are no higher than permits an average man to stand upright inside, while the floor space can little more than accommodate two or three outstretched forms. Gipsy-like, they are not in any degree extravagant in labour of construction or in expenditure of material, from which it may be gathered that the natives are lazy and material scarce.

There are a number of stone-built dwellings at Tasessat and elsewhere, but nowhere are they occupied by the natives, who have allowed them to relapse to a state of ruin. Whether those strange old dwellings belonged to a race which at one time the Tuaregs conquered, or to their own ancestors, I do not know, though I am inclined to think that they are of Hausa origin. At all events, they belong solely to the Past, when, at some time or other, there were many people in the Baguezan mountains, for in numerous places are to be found the old sites of villages where huts were built of stone: in some cases the whole village completely overthrown, in others a few skeletons of huts standing. Also there are many strange old graveyards, sometimes near an old village site, sometimes where no sign of dwelling-place remains. They are usually on a level stony piece of ground, chosen, I surmise, because jackals cannot scrape down through such a surface, and the graves, which have lain there through ages, are still marked with mounds of pebbles heaped body-length, or with borders of selected stones laid out in the shape of a coffin; while in some cases the wood poles, which support the stones laid over the grave, have given out, and the grave lies partly open.

The natives of to-day point to ruins of this kind, and tell, with a very real ring of sadness in their voices, that they mark the full and awful extent of decline in population—the ravages of war and the pillage at the hands of raiders who, even to-day, descend upon the hapless decadent people to steal their camels and take their young men and women into slavery.

Minerou and the old headman of Tasessat declare that natives of Baguezan of the present time have not fled or been driven to the low country in the south. Such a thing could not possibly be, they say, "for there are no mountains there, and how could we live without them?"—true mountain people, the land of their birth dear to their hearts as their freedom.

To-day there are altogether only 40 male Tuaregs in Baguezan mountains; that is, adult men at the head of a family.

According to native statement, there has never been, in living memory, an English-speaking white man in Baguezan before; and no one, they say, has camped or roamed about the hills as I have done, in which event I trust this humble description of the place may hold some particular interest. Old natives say that, previous to my visit, there have been, in all, three white men in Baguezan: French officers who have had occasion to enter Baguezan in course of performing duty, and who did not remain there any length of time.

The natives of Baguezan, like all natives of Aïr, get the grain which is their principal food chiefly from Tanout and district, a journey of about 496 miles altogether, outward and homeward. It is transported by caravans of camels. On some occasions the natives carry south with them, to market, dates, which they get chiefly from Fachi, but a few from Aïr, and goat hides. Fachi, and also Bilma, are oases on the desert east of Aïr. Fachi, according to the natives, is fifteen days' caravan journey from Baguezan, and Bilma 30 days' journey. Both places are very well known to the natives of the territory, for it is chiefly from those places that they obtain salt for themselves and their camels.

With regard to the climate of Baguezan, the inhabitants say that they have no snow in the mountains at any time, but there is ice in the cold season (about November). Personally I have witnessed a shower of large hailstones in Baguezan, similar to occurrences of the kind witnessed in South Africa and during a Canadian summer, when such hail-showers sometimes fall in the course of a particularly violent thunderstorm. To one who comes from the stifling hot desert, the remarkable clearness of the air of Baguezan gives untold delight, while the coolness of morning and evening in the mountains goes far toward reviving drooping vitality. In my case I often look back and doubt if I could have completed the undertaking without a disastrous breakdown had I not had the good fortune to pick up a new store of vigour during my stay among the mountain-tops of Baguezan.

I noted the following temperatures during the month of May: daybreak, 60°, 62°, 68°, 74° Fahr.; noon, 96° Fahr.; sundown, 80°, 76°, 74° Fahr.

I hope to describe the Tuaregs of Aïr in a later chapter, and for the moment, so far as the natives of Baguezan are concerned, may briefly say that they are true mountain people, not very tall, sturdily built, strong in wind and limb, and extraordinarily active in hill-climbing. But they are cunning, shifty, and suspicious people, and I never felt I was made a friend among them; and Baguezan, up to the present, ranks as the one place where I have felt frustrated in overtures toward friendship with the local inhabitants. I hunted in Baguezan from 6th May to 7th June, but my feeling of insecurity may be judged in that I pitched camp well apart from the village of Tasessat and surrounded it with a strong thorn zereba, through which no one could enter without disturbance, and never lay down at night without my loaded rifle by my side.

I consider I had only one friend in Baguezan: a native who might be called the local smith, for he handled a bellows that nourished a coke fire and welded primitive tools and weapons and trinkets for the people. He often came to my camp uncalled, and gladly did me any service that I wished that was within his power. Next to him I trusted most the chief, Minerou; principally because I knew him well—his good points and his faults. With him I was friends, at least outwardly—as friendly as one can be with a person shrewdly suspected of being an unscrupulous rascal. The commandant at Agades, replying to a letter of mine from Baguezan, wrote with regard to Minerou: "Yes! the Chief of Baguezan is underneath full of slyness: and so they all are. But you know the bush law better than myself, and I rely upon your carefully watching. Don't trust any of them."

I find in my diary the following notes of the Chief of Baguezan: "Among his people he is a king, and all appear to obey his command. How he obtains authority over his wild-natured flock is, to me, mysterious, yet the power of king is his. He is wise in a cunning way, and appears to have greater capacity for enterprise and work than any of his people. Like all Tuaregs, he has no subterfuge in his greed for food or clothing or money. He professes to be my friend, yet at heart I know he is full of suspicion of the stranger, and is friends, in reality, only with my purse, and, also, because he fears the military authorities at Agades. In his religion, Mohammedan, or sect of Mohammedan, he is very devout, and at sunrise or sunset, no matter what occupation he may interrupt, he never fails to address his incantations and salaams to the east; and I would not be surprised if the excessive zeal of his devotion induces the belief that his faith is supreme, and shuts out the white man as a fanatic or an enemy to his God."

In time the period of hunting among the Baguezan mountains came to an end, and I turned my thoughts to travelling northward, an undertaking not altogether looked on with favour by the authorities at Agades, who, though desirous of helping me, declared, like the natives, that the journey entailed, perhaps, foolish risk. My own view of the matter is partly contained in the following letter to the commandant at Agades: ". . . with regard to going further north, I place myself entirely in your hands, knowing you will advise me for the best and assist me where you can. I realise even here that there is risk and that one must ever be careful and on the alert, but nothing worth while was ever accomplished without overcoming difficulties, and I would much like, since I have come so far with that purpose, to complete my journey fully in Aïr. From my map I estimate that Aguellal is 4 to 5 days further north and Iferouan 1 to 2 days more (Iferouan would be the end of my northward journey), while outward or homeward I would like to visit Assodé. I purpose travelling very light, and estimate that 3 or 4 camels would suffice for the journey. Regarding escort, I leave the matter entirely with you, who know conditions much better than I do. For my own part, I am ready to undertake any risk, but any natives who may accompany me might feel reassured with a small show of rifles. This is a type of mountain country where but a few armed men could put up a great fight—if not taken by surprise in the dark. But now there is the chief point: to obtain one native who knows where there is water to be found on the journey. The Chief of Baguezan declares none of his people know the north territory, though I doubt his statement, and strongly suspect it is prompted by the universal fear of entering an ill-reputed neighbourhood. Possibly a guide can be secured in Agades? Where men from the north are to be found, you, of course, know, and in this, as in everything, I will await your consideration of the matter and your advice."

Which letter brought satisfactory results; so that on the afternoon of 7th June I was able to commence the journey to Iferouan, situated in the extreme north of Aïr.

CHAPTER XII
THE NORTHERN REGIONS OF AÏR: PART I

O N 6th June I received a letter from the commandant at Agades suggesting that I proceed at once on my contemplated journey to the northern regions of Aïr, proposing that I push forward under conditions that would restrict the time that I remain beyond communication with Agades to a period of 15 days. This was short time indeed for the journey, and would entail constant travelling, but I had no wish to question the desire of the French authorities, who, with kindness and courtesy, assisted me in every way in their power to make the expedition a success; therefore, to this proposal I at once concurred, and sent back a message to say that if all went well, news of me might be expected at Agades not later than 23rd June.

At the same time I was advised that six goumiers, to join me at Timia, would be despatched from Agades on the following day, which, with Atagoom and Saidi (the goumiers already with me) and myself, would make up a party of nine rifles for the journey. Atagoom and Saidi, who had now been with me for more than a month, had become very friendly, and had grown familiar with the white man's ways, so that I was particularly glad that they were available for the forthcoming journey. They were, like all Tuaregs, very lazy when about camp, but splendid camel-men and travellers when once out on the trail, Atagoom in particular being an exceptionally active and tireless individual.

At the last moment, when loading up the camels in preparation to depart from Baguezan, the Chief offered me a man to look after my camels on the way to Timia; a powerfully built fellow, bigger than the average native of Aïr, and appropriately named Dogo, which is Hausa for tall, though he was more often addressed as Buzu, the Tamāshack for slave—for such he was, free to all outward appearance, but bound to the service of the Chief in some mysterious way and dependent upon him. This man, like so many others, was not a pure-blooded Tuareg— probably not of Tuareg descent at all, for he was a descendant of slaves—although he spoke their language and dressed as they did. He was a remarkably reticent individual, and never spoke a word to me unless I first addressed him, when he would couch his answer in a few brief syllables, and then shut up like a clam. I give those few particulars of Dogo because, although he set out merely to accompany me to Timia, he came forward a couple of days later and voluntarily offered to go the journey north with me: which he did, and thenceforward this strange fellow, who never gave outward demonstration of human feeling, attached himself devotedly to my caravan (with the consent of the Chief), and looked after the camels during all subsequent travel in Aïr, and, in the end, accompanied me all the way back to Kano. Which was great good fortune for me, for he was a splendid worker, and soon grew familiar with the animals and their burdens, the way in which I liked to load up or off-load, his duties in camp, and in tending the camels when turned out to graze, so that in time I needed to pay little attention to him, feeling secure that no detail would be forgotten.

We left Tasessat about 2 p.m. on 7th June, and travelled over the plateau in a north-westerly direction, heading for the Pass that gave exit to Timia. Our route over the plateau was far from a direct one, since it was necessary to dodge in and out to evade the numerous hills, while it was over cruelly rough country almost altogether of stones and rocks, which punished the camels' feet severely; so severely that, after an equally hard journey the following day, one of the animals had to be discarded when reaching Timia. We were still on the plateau at sundown, and camped about an hour's journey from the head of the Pass.

Next day travel was resumed, and we soon came to the top of the pass, where a magnificent view from the mountain edge lay before us of the wide gradient of the rough hill-covered Baguezan mountain sides, and of the very broad valley which lay westwards between us and the Béla mountains, and is drained northward in time of rain by the Assada river and its numerous tributaries.

Throughout the day I was delighted and astonished by the wealth of everchanging scene of mountain and hill and valley, hardly finishing appreciation of one striking picture before it changed, as we moved onward, and another came into view to arrest attention. (To my mind, wild mountain scenery, second only to the magnificent views which surround Timia, is here seen at its best in Aïr—a region rich in mountain landscape.) In the Infinite Detail I found greatest attraction, detail of constant change of form and contour, and perspective of country full of rugged features. It is not scene that is rich in colour, being overclouded with the dominant dull greyness of the bare rock and stone, and therefore, perhaps, contains no great appeal to one who might appraise it with the eye of a painter; rather would I suggest that it holds appeal for the etcher, insomuch that there is such a wealth of detail, detail delicate or superbly masterful, in form and outline, in grotesque shapes, and in strength of shadow.

So far as travel underfoot was concerned, we put in a long arduous day, first descending the pass out of Baguezan, which is a more rugged and difficult one than that in the south, and then continuing among foothills that never offered a level course, so that we were constantly climbing or descending rocky, stony hill-ground or dipping into the numerous ravines that crossed our path; and we were still about a day's journey from Timia when we camped at night.

Before dawn on the following day—9th June— we had risen from our hard beds on the open ground (I had left all camp equipment in Baguezan, so that this journey should not be unnecessarily hampered with baggage) and pushed on to Timia, which it was necessary we should reach this day, for we had been unable to find water at sundown yesterday, and had almost finished the store in our goat-skin bags.

Daylight found us slowly advancing northward, in towards Agalak mountains, which loomed massively in a long line before us; at first dimly, haze-softened, then growing to a frowning countenance, in which cliffs and clefts and precipitous ravines could be discerned. By which time we began to swing easterly, keeping the slopes of Agalak mountains, which appear to have a plateau summit, not far distant on our left, while Baguezan mountains lay almost out of sight on our right. About 11 o'clock, after toiling up and down dale, over stone-strewn ground and among rocks that presented difficulty to free travel as constantly as yesterday, we emerged on to a wide river-bed of loose sand which bore the name of Abarakan in the locality where we intersected it. Still heading east, we continued up the river course for a long time in the full heat of day and with the sun-glare rebounding off the sand, which was very loose and powdery, as in all river-beds in Aïr, and heavy underfoot for the camels, but vastly better than the terrible mountain trail we had left behind. About 1.30 p.m. we branched off the river, ascending the right bank on to a small level stony plain which lay beneath the western slopes of some low hills near to and S.E. of the Timia range. We crossed this plain in a northerly direction, into which course the river had also turned just about the time we parted from it, and even now the river channel was not far distant on our left, drawing a parallel line also to Timia, but not so directly as the one which Dogo, the local native, was following. However, at the head of the rocky plain, where it terminated at the foot of hills which shut it in completely, we again intercepted the river, about 2 miles from Timia, where precipitous slopes dipped to the very edge of the east bank and completely blocked passage on that side. Hence we entered the river-bed again, and travelled up it a little way, between steep banks, until we came to the mouth of Timia Gorge, and encountered the strange and formidable barrier that there shuts off further progress up the river. This obstacle was the sheer cliff of a dry waterfall of height of some 25 to 30 ft., and, in conjunction with the closely crowding hill-sides on either bank, it appeared to close the narrow neck between the hills altogether. But native wit, or necessity, had found a way to force a door in the barrier, to give passage to caravans into the rich gorge that lay beyond, for close examination of the west bank of the river reveals a winding, precipitous, cave-like staircase hewn out of the solid rock, which ascends to the top of the high bank, where there is space enough, and no more, between mountain base and river-bank, to allow camels to pass above the fall. One by one we led each camel into this stairway, which they had to strain and struggle to ascend, and humoured them slowly upwards, until all were safely at the top, when we proceeded up the broad river-bed into Timia without further hindrance.

Timia Gorge is, in my opinion, the most beautiful spot in Aïr and the most fertile. It has a length of some three or four miles, through which the wide shallow river-bed winds (I judge the river to be 75 to 100 yards wide), while the steep slopes of the majestic heights of Agalak and Timia mountains descend on either side to its very margin, leaving, in places, narrow little stretches of ground upon the banks, no wider than a mansion garden, which are irrigated by means of wells and cultivated by the natives to grow wheat and millet and maize, or bear thick groves of date palms.

We entered Timia village about 4 p.m., and were warmly welcomed by the fine old headman, who acted as deputy in absence of the Chief Fougda. I was amused to find that, as in many other instances, all the natives who gathered around while we off-loaded already knew of me and wanted to look on "the hunting white man," while many of the women and children of the village, who did not travel to Agades like the men, had never seen a European before, and were vastly interested in a timid, furtive way.

I was greatly pleased with Timia village, which is built chiefly on the west bank of the river in a small open flat stony pocket at the eastern base of Agalak. The small dome dwellings are the same as those on Baguezan, but built with more care, while there is a decided appearance of neatness and tidiness in the whole village which I found lacking elsewhere in inhabited places in Aïr. Moreover, I found the people really industrious in working their riverside gardens, and, in fact, when I came to see more of them a week or two later, I judged them to be the most superior tribe I had encountered in Aïr.

The six goumiers from Agades joined me at Timia, heavily masked, like all Tuaregs, with yashmak, which leaves only the eyes uncovered, and picturesquely dressed in cotton robes of various colours; while the old headman brought forward a young fellow named Homa, who had been born in Iferouan and was to act as guide, and, in particular, point out where water was to be found. He and another man had been part of the way north about a month before trying to trap donkeys, which escaped from the natives at the time of the evacuations, or out of the hands of robbers, and are now running completely wild in Aïr. (Later I saw fresh tracks of one band, and many signs of them where they had been feeding.) Those men succeeded in trapping one donkey, but say the brutes are terribly wild and difficult to catch.

The altitude of the stream-bed at Timia village is 3,800 feet, while some of the splendid tops of Timia mountains, which are higher than Agalak (map alt.: 4,593 ft.), appear to be easily 2,000 to 3,000 ft. more, and it would not surprise me if the highest altitude in Aïr is contained in Timia mountains, and I regret I had not occasion or time to climb to the highest peak.

Next morning, 10th June, we left Timia and started on the long journey north in uninhabited regions. In the early part of the day we travelled over rough, broken, rocky country until Tiggeur was reached, the abandoned site of a village (alt. 3,700 ft.), where there are a few date palms and an old well which contains no water. To the east the country had appeared more open thus far, and contained a number of small hills, while on the west lay the high slopes of Agalak mountains. Thereafter we continued by Tiggeur and Teguednu river-beds, which had bare, almost treeless banks, and camped at the junction where the latter stream and the Asselar meet and become the broad Agoras river-bed, which trends away N.W. to the ancient town of Assodé. Altitude at this camping-place, 3,150 ft.

To-night and henceforth a sentry was posted and the camels made to lie down in a half-circle, while the goumiers slept beside them, so that we were prepared in the event of robbers stealing in upon us.

11th June.—Slight rain in early part of night; otherwise no disturbance. Woke once or twice, hearing the sentry moving about in idle wakefulness, which recalled habits of active service.

Left our night camping-place about an hour before dawn and travelled to Igouloulof. To-day we passed through country more open in expanse, not in general so mountainous as hitherto, which contained in the rough lowlands some level stretches of sand and stone, while Goundaï mountains loomed large and very conspicuous at a distance to the east.

Igouloulof (altitude, 2,950 ft.), on the north bank of a sandy river-bed that trends east, proved to be a small deserted village among rocks composed of remarkably well-built, flat-roofed stone huts, which are whitish-grey in colour owing to the use of a natural cement in their construction, apparently obtained from open pits in the village. The huts bear a strange aspect against the black rocks, showing like little square pill-boxes inset here and there with pleasing irregularity. They are built without system in laying the stone—no rubble, no regular jointing, just a jumble of stones that are not very large, set in a liberal bed of mortar.

Such places, now deserted—and there are many in Aïr—fill me with sadness; they are often in pleasant situations, and picturesque even now, notwithstanding the strange bleakness and stillness of the land, but one cannot refrain from thinking how much more attractive Aïr would be if occupied by happy natives, and a wayfarer could see, instead of this melancholy desolation, smoke of wood-fires rising and hear homely sounds.

It is difficult to ascertain from the natives, with any certainty of accuracy, the period when Aïr first began to decline in population, though, of course, they all know of the final desertion which took place, about three years ago, in the forced evacuations following on the Rebellion of 1916, when the remnants of the Tuareg inhabitants were commanded by the French authorities to settle in the neighbourhood of Agades under direct protection of the Fort and within reach of surveillance. But this last was a comparatively small affair, and does not by any means account for the loss of the large population, which, if one is to judge by the numerous ruins of old villages and graveyards, once occupied the Aïr mountains. Apart from the question of the extent of oppression pursued by stronger tribes from outside territories, I am prone to wonder if Aïr has undergone any great geological change or climatic change which has made it less fertile than hitherto? For it seems to me that want and hunger are the most tangible causes that drive people to forsake dearthful country and seek a better elsewhere capable of supporting livelihood; more especially if the people happen to be, as in Aïr, naturally nomadic. I think it may be accepted that Aïr in the present age is a land of dearth not capable of supporting a great many people. If it was a rich land, and war was the great scourge that destroyed the people, would not the victors seize the country and settle in it? Such thoughts naturally occur to me, because I cannot believe that this dreadfully bare country, as it is to-day, ever offered any inducement to a large population to live in it; while if food for many people was carried from Damergou, Damagarim, and Kano in the south, it must have constituted a colossal and unending task that necessitated the upkeep of great herds of camels and an abundant growth of forage: viz. grass, ground plants, acacias, "Abisgee," and other bushes.

Therefore the solution may lie in geological change or climatic change, such as may have altered the whole aspect of the land's fertility. If sands have swept in from the desert seas that bound Aïr, to pile up gradually at the base of the range through centuries of time and smother forests of acacia and other plant life which may have been there, then the land has suffered a great loss (I have crossed the edge of the eastern plain below Baguezan mountains, where there are still considerable numbers of acacias close in to the margin where mountain rock terminates); while also the sand that is blown into the mountains from the desert is, during Rains, washed into the valleys and innumerable river-beds, causing, perhaps, the valleys to grow in depth of sand and the rivers, for lack of sufficient gradient, or by reason of an estuary out on the desert that may be slowly blocking up, to gradually fill up and choke, where once, perhaps, there were deep rocky channels which held pools of water all the year round.

If, on the other hand, or also, climatic conditions have changed, and much less rain falls now than in former years— natives declare some years in the present are practically rainless—the difference in the fertility of the country would be tremendous, for Aïr, with its countless river-courses, under conditions of bountiful lasting rainfall would be rich and beautiful indeed.

12th June.—Bad weather set in last evening, beginning with rapidly rising gale; then developing to thunderstorm and rain. Heavy rain fell through the night, and we slept in water-soaked blankets.

We left Igouloulof at daybreak, and continued northward to Faodet. During the morning we passed through some broad valley country, where evergreen "Abisgee" bushes were fairly numerous, in locality the guide called "Tchyerus"; and the river of that name, draining westwards (which appears to be a local name for a section of the Zilalet river, which is an arm of the great Agoras), was forded, as it was in flood after the rain of last night. Thereafter, before coming to Agarageur, we passed over open country of pale sand, dotted with small cone-shaped hills, which opened up in wide expanse westward. Agarageur mountain was passed close on our right, and the stone-built village of Afis, which is S.W. of the range, the tiny dwellings, strikingly diminutive, tucked in at the great mountain base. Agarageur mountain (named Tamgak on Courtier's French map, but called by the natives Agarageur) appears high and stately, rising in rugged slopes from massive boulder-strewn base. Altitude at foot of Agarageur, 2,600 ft.

Approaching Faodet, where we camped, we travelled among rough foothills, with the large magnificent range of the same name on the east. The village of Faodet is in a level sand-basin, which contains some "Abisgee" and acacia trees and an old deep well, which is in bad disrepair and long out of use. The deserted stone dwellings lie back among the foothills in a pleasant ravine. The altitude at Faodet is 2,900 ft.

Not long before reaching Faodet, a fierce thunderstorm burst, and we were suddenly caught on a bare hill-crest by onslaught of heavy driving torrential rain, and as camels will not face such weather, they at once turned their backs to the biting gale and slashing rain, and huddled together in little groups to stand motionless with their cowering, unprotected riders on their backs, while the rain beat down on them. It was a strange sight—groups drawn together for protection, patiently waiting, the rain, as if incensed, literally hurling itself angrily down upon us in torrents, while the ground at our feet grew to a flowing stream of water, and camels shifted their feet uneasily as the wet and discomfort and cold increased. But in the end, as always in this country, the brief mad storm ceased, and we shook out our bedraggled feathers, so to speak, and journeyed on our way.

We had barely restarted when a second unexpected incident surprised us this day; and this was when breasting a ridge we came right on top of three men ascending from the other side. Their appearance was extraordinary: they were clothed solely in skins of wild sheep and gazelle, and their whole colour, even to their pale light yellowish faces, was a remarkable blend with the sand. Had we not surprised them, it is certain that we should never have detected them hidden away among rocks and sand. They were absolutely wild men of the mountains, roaming those uninhabited ranges at will, and were amazed and visibly frightened when finding themselves completely at our mercy; which fear was partly dispelled when they were told I had no wish to make captives of them or harm them. They all carried short wooden-shafted spears, and bundles of skin bags containing their scant belongings, slung over their shoulders on a short stick; one also carried a small child perched on the top of his shoulder and clinging to the crown of his head. All were wearing yashmaks, which veiled their faces in the usual Tuareg fashion. When it was found that we were friendly, two women were revealed concealed fearfully among the rocks near by, and with them were four small naked children—two of them infants in arms. Those strange people had no goats and no grain, and were living on wild meat, which they trapped with snares, green barely ripe dates, and edible roots and leaves and berries of worth known to themselves. They had not been out of Tamgak mountains for a year, they declared, and were on their way to Igouloulof to gather "Abisgee" berries, now ripening in that district. I gave them half a gazelle, killed this day, and sent them gratefully on their way, letting them go, knowing they might never be seen again, with the same feelings as I might liberate snared animals, and watch them bound away into the wilderness, their dearly loved freedom regained.

WILD MEN, NORTHERN AÏR.

APPROACHING IFEROUAN.

I note to-day that thus far no mosquitoes, which had appeared further south in the wake of the first light Rains, have been seen north of Timia.

Shot three Dorcas Gazelles to-day to augment our food supplies; a number of those animals seen.

Each day I note down the few birds which I see, and remain watchful for new species which I may not have already collected in Aïr; but up to now have found nothing of that kind.

13th June.—Leaving Faodet, a broad view of mountain range was sighted soon after daylight to the north and east, and the slopes and outline of the great Tamgak mountains, in the north of Aïr, lay before us, not in appearance of astonishing height (map alt. west side of range 5,569 ft.), but very rugged and of massive solidity, for they are of extensive area. But before the Tamgak range is reached, a very wide valley or flat sandy plain is crossed which lies between the Faodet mountains and Tamgak mountains. At this time we could see in the north a peculiar blunt-pointed isolated tower of rock projecting above the most distant mountains in sight along the Tamgak range, which the guide at once declared denoted the position of Iferouan; and once one has seen this unique rock spire from the south, or anywhere, one could never mistake the locality of Iferouan in the whole of Aïr. (It transpired later that this spire is nearer to Zeloufiet than Iferouan, for we swung out in a north-west direction from the mountains at Zeloufiet, to find Iferouan in a wide fertile valley at a considerable distance from Tamgak.) Thus, in the morning, we sighted a landmark of our destination, which we expected to reach about 4 p.m.

Crossing the flat sandy plain, referred to above, the village of Iberkom was found right in under mountain slopes of Tamgak, in a valley fertile in open bush growth, which was already pleasantly green from the fall of recent rain. There were some date palms at Iberkom and a few stone huts among the bare rocks.

Leaving Iberkom, we followed round the western base of Tamgak range, crossing over one or two bare rocky ridges, but generally following along the narrow level bush-grown sandy valley that circled round the base of the towering grey rocks. We next passed a small village named Tanetmolet, deserted like all others, with a well which contained no water. Altitude, 2,400 ft. Soon afterwards Tintaghoda was passed: a picturesque widely laid out village on a gravel ridge, the stone huts of which were more elaborate than any seen elsewhere, having roof parapets and craftless ornament in some cases, while all buildings were of peculiar colouring, since the stones were laid in a brick-red mortar. (I did not dismount and walk about the empty village, which I much regretted afterwards, when I learned, from the exiled Chief of Iferouan, that this place contains an important mosque. On the other hand I had been told that there was a mosque at Iferouan, and could find no trace of it there, and now know that the Tintaghoda mosque is the one of the territory.) A deep well south of the village held water in plenty, but it was sour and stagnant from lying long unused.

The bush-grown valley narrowed after we had breasted the stony rise of Tintaghoda, then opened out again before Zeloufiet is reached; another village that is first viewed on a bare stony ridge, and of some picturesqueness and variety when entered, except that it is sadly desolate like all the others. There is a fine belt of date palms to the west of the huts, and many old garden-patches which still bear the marks of irrigation, at one time laid out with the purpose of nursing cultivation. At Zeloufiet the great Tamgak mountains have died down, and the wide flat basin, wherein is the village, is surrounded by ranges of low black hills; while the strange rock spire, which we had seen from afar in the morning, lies due east of the village. Between Zeloufiet and Iferouan the shallow, bankless river we have been keeping in touch with in the bush-grown valley along the mountain base broadens out and becomes the extremely wide shallow Igheser river-bed, which on its banks carry some dum palms and date palms, besides some "Abisgee" and acacia bush; while the small villages of Afassat and Tassebet, which each contain some date palms, are passed on the east bank of the river before Iferouan is reached.

Nearing Iferouan, the goumiers were much interested in the tracks of a single camel in the sand of the river-bed. Expert in reading the minutest detail of any individual camel track, they spent some time following the signs, which led toward Iferouan, and conjecturing among themselves over them. They were not very fresh tracks, a week or ten days old, but the natives decided that they were certainly the marks of a camel from the north; no doubt the mount of a scout from some Hogar band of robbers sent to spy out the land: looking at the dates in Iferouan to judge, perhaps, when they would be ripe, so that they might, in season, be plundered or descent be planned upon the people who might be sent from Timia or Agades to gather them—a disaster which actually occurred last year. On the other hand, the outlaw might have gone into Iferouan for water, and thereafter proceeded south to spy about the borders of inhabited districts to seek out the grazing-places of camels, with a view to his band swooping in on them and bearing them off; as so often happens in Aïr in the present day.

It was a weary band of men, and camels, that off-loaded and camped in Iferouan, for we had travelled hard for the last few days over country that held many drawbacks to comfortable travel.

The dwellings of Iferouan are on the west bank of the Igheser river, among, and bordering, an extensive date-palm and dum-palm belt, where many wells are sunk which once served the wants of natives and irrigated the garden patches, that had evidently been cultivated on every available piece of ground within the palm grove. (Later the exiled Chief of Iferouan, by name Obidelkilli, informed me that it was principally wheat which was grown there in the past, a grain which in all probability came into the country from northern Africa.) The huts in the palm grove are of cane framework and grass thatched, and are chiefly in a state of ruin, while outside the grove, on the margin of stony ground to the west, there are both grass huts and stone huts. Also, on an island, quite apart from the village, out in the centre of the wide stream-bed, there is a small house of European aspect, apparently a small post or place of accommodation for resident or visiting French officer at one time.

From Iferouan one views the rugged western slopes of the great Tamgak range out to the northern extreme, and low hills beyond that tail away in the distance—the last of the hills of Aïr, broken hills that appear to grow more diminutive and scattered as they recede beyond the care of the wild mountain ranges of Aïr. . . . I had reached my goal, the north of Aïr, a goal which from the time I left England to this memorable day had never been promised with any measure of certainty; and perhaps I may be forgiven if at this hour I was filled with gladness.

CHAPTER XIII
THE NORTHERN REGIONS OF AÏR: PART II

I REMAINED the next day in Iferouan collecting a few specimens of doves, inhabiting the palm trees, which proved to be *Streptopelia turtur hoggara*, a rare and beautiful soft-coloured richly mottled dove which I found in no other locality in Aïr. This was the first and only good find during my northern journey, throughout which birds remained remarkably scarce. I think, after all, birds like the society of mankind; at any rate, desolate, man-forsaken northern Aïr held very few birds indeed in comparison with inhabited districts in the south. Mankind cultivate seed crops, keep herds of cattle, throw out debris, live where water is to be found, and have a score or more habits, each of which unconsciously, in some way, is of benefit to one or other of the feathered tribe.

I did not intend to return to Timia by the route I had come, but to journey south-west to Aguellal, the most western mountain range in Aïr of any importance, and thence cut back eastward by way of the ancient town of Assodé.

Before setting out, an unexpected difficulty cropped up in that, wilfully or truthfully, Homa, the native who had been guide to Iferouan, declared that he did not know the way to Aguellal. I had made my plans quite clear before leaving Timia, and was considerably annoyed to find that I had been misled as to the ability of the guide. I called the goumiers, and asked each one if he knew the country, but received a negative reply from all, which, so far as I could judge, was true, although by this time I knew something of Tuareg shortcomings, and was aware that the whole business might be a ruse to put me off returning by a circuitous and longer route. In any case, I nipped any indecision, which they may have wished to encourage, in the bud, by declaring emphatically that I had a good *Takarda* (map), and would lead the way to Aguellal, at the same time knowing the men would have to accompany me unless they wished to greatly displease their officer at Agades.

My map showed a track from Iferouan to Aguellal, and the evening before starting I sent the chief goumier and Homa out to search for it west of the village. They came back at dark with the encouraging news that they had found a track out on the stony plain leading westward.

Hence at daybreak on 15th June we set out from Iferouan in the direction of Aguellal. The track soon proved to be very vague, so that I had to refer frequently to map and compass before Aguellal mountain range loomed in sight, a procedure which astonished and impressed the natives, who had for days past been vastly interested in the magic sheet of paper which told me so much about a land which they were aware I had never seen before. From time to time we picked up the old track, usually on stony ground where sand had not drifted, and thus reassured we kept on a true course.

The country between Iferouan and Aguellal is in general aspect plain-like and expansive and very barren. Low rugged hills lie west and south of Iferouan, in country of alternating stretches of light gravel and sand in slight hollows and valleys, and darker gravel and rock on the rounded ridges and higher lands. When more than midway on our journey, we crossed an extensive sandy plain on its western margin, and there the old track was completely obliterated by weather and drifting sand, and I noticed the leading camel-man was following, at times, the small particles of bleached camel-litter of animals that had long ago passed this way—in the end, even those slight signs, that would escape unpractised eyes, were lost.

No trees were seen to-day, except an occasional low weed-like, ill-nourished bush and a few scattered acacias at our night camp, which was chosen in the Aniogaran valley bed (altitude, 2,200 ft.), at which time we were in full view of the northern slopes of rugged Aguellal.

Dr. Barth, on entering the Aïr mountains from the north in 1850, described the approach to Aguellal as "a picturesque wilderness," where "majestic mountains and detached peaks towered over the landscape."

Unlike other localities throughout to-day's journey, there was no sign of recent rainfall, and the land lay terribly parched, and altogether the most drear and barren area we had entered since leaving Timia.

The undulating fairly level type of country was of the type favoured by Dorcas Gazelles, and a number of them were seen to-day, and an animal shot for food.

I am now living principally on buck-meat and dried dates bought in Timia, for my European stores, which I have had to draw on heavily ever since leaving the inhabited regions of Damergou, are almost finished. The articles I miss most of all, and which ran out about a month ago, are sugar and tobacco; especially the latter, which can be a wonderful solace when the palate grows listless on a constant diet of freshly killed meat.

Resuming the journey on the following day, we changed our course westward and then southward, to swing round the north-west spur of the Aguellal range, over very rough foothills, through which an old mountain track led us in toward Aguellal village, which lay hidden round the corner of the spur, until we came suddenly in sight of it at close range.

We camped in Aguellal two hours after setting out. Aguellal village (altitude, 2,100 ft.) is beneath the western slope of the strange dark mountains of the same name—magnificent ranges in rugged contour, and of considerable height— while westward from the deserted village, or rather, villages, for there are four separate groups of dwellings in different localities, stretches a wide sandy valley, with green banks of low bush comprised chiefly of "Abisgee" and acacia. There are no date palms at Aguellal and no old signs of grain cultivation; indeed, I doubt if the barren stony ground would permit of cultivation. So that natives in the past apparently gave their attention entirely to maintaining herds of goats and camels, though, in general, Aguellal mountain has little attractive fertility round its base, and is surrounded by country of more barren appearance than the more central ranges,[10] which have a certain fertility in some of the valleys in their immediate surroundings.

The deserted huts in the villages are stone-built and of reddish colour, and many contained relics of native furniture and utensils, such as wooden stools, mortar bowls, grass mats, grass-made baskets and dishes, and earthenware water-jars. In a number of dwellings jars were found built into the inside walls, and the goumiers informed me that those were customarily used by natives as hiding-places for money.

There is a deep well at Aguellal in the centre of the principal village.

Accompanied by Atagoom and Saidi, I left camp not long after midday, and proceeded to climb into Aguellal mountains, an undertaking which proved to be a strenuous one, and we did not get back to camp until after dark. Mountain climbing in intense heat is not mountain climbing under ideal conditions, and we put in an afternoon of extreme exertion, for Aguellal slopes are very steep, almost cliff-like in their upper reaches, and of a rugged composition which rendered them quite impassable in places. We succeeded, before receding daylight warned us to begin descent, in climbing to a summit which registered 3,100 ft., 1,000 ft. above Aguellal village, which is a very considerable distance away from the actual mountain base. Other peaks were, at that altitude, above us north and south-west, which appeared almost inaccessible without the aid of ropes, and I judged they might have additional height of 600 to 800 ft. (On one map which I possess there is an altitude reading on the east side of the range of 3,609 ft.)

Fresh tracks of wild sheep were numerous in the mountain.

17th June.—Left Aguellal at daybreak, travelling first south-west to avoid the southern spur of Aguellal, and thereafter swinging round into the south-east with the intention of cutting in to the broad Agoras valley, and thence continuing up the river course to Assodé. The journey to-day was the hardest performed since leaving Timia, being throughout over rocky, irregular lowland, which offered bad foothold for the camels and entailed much variance of direction to avoid impassable rocks and gully channels. Throughout the day there were many individual hills in the landscape. About mid-journey a long time was spent in making our way through the strange pass that is between the large detached hills of Matalgha and Marasset—a much greater time and distance than the map would lead one to expect.

Marasset is prominent, and can be identified a long way off. It has one peak in particular, which rises high above all else and terminates in twin cone-shaped towers.

IN AGUELLAL MOUNTAINS AT 3,100 FEET.

WE FIND A PRECIOUS POOL OF WATER
S.E. OF AGUELLAL, AÏR.

Beyond Marasset we found a pool of fresh rainwater, which brought forth a general exclamation of pleasure, while halt was made to slack our immediate thirst and fill all our water-skins. Throughout this journey in northern Aïr it has been, excepting on one other occasion, our lot to subsist on the stagnant, foul-tasted waters obtained from old decayed village wells which have not been in use for some years.

We camped about 4 p.m. at a small village named Ebazouera, near to the edge of the expansive Agoras valley; a tiny village containing a few ruins and three standing stone huts. There was no well. Altitude, 2,300 ft.

18th June.—About two hours after setting out in the early morning we passed out of rocky land and intersected the Agoras river, which was then followed upstream until Assodé was reached about 2 p.m. The river-bed of sand is very wide, with shallow banks almost barren of trees. It was necessary for me to act as guide, as on the previous days; moreover, the natives now had implicit faith in my magic *Takarda* (map). One might think that doubt should not arise travelling in a wide river-bed, nevertheless it does; broad channels open up in the shores, outlets of other streams join into the Agoras, and more than once the question arises: which shall be followed of two broad ways?—which seem, at their junction, to both lead much in the same direction. However, when nearing Assodé, one or two of the goumiers, and the guide Homa, began to find landmarks with which they were familiar, and I soon learned that I need have no further concern as to our whereabouts, as the way back to Timia was henceforth known to the natives.

I may say that the French map of Aïr, resultant from the Cortier Geographical Mission, which had been kindly given to me at Agades, proved of the utmost service to me throughout my travels in Aïr, and is an excellent and accurate map if one follows it on broadly conceived lines. But one must form conception of proportion very expansively, for the scale (and, perhaps, the extent of geographical data) does not permit the inclusion of the abundant detail which this rugged mountain-land possesses. For instance, the chief mountain ranges and a great many hills and rivers are indicated, but there are hundreds, yea, perhaps, thousands, of individual hills and many streams which are not included on the map.

The village or town of Assodé (altitude, 2,475 ft.) is the largest I came across in Aïr north of Agades. It is strangely situated in a small stony plateau-basin, behind high rocky banks on the north side of the Agoras river, in country more hilly than that which borders the river further west. The basin, wherein lies the village, is completely surrounded with natural ramparts of small hills, and therefore presents the appearance of a place capable of strong defence in time of war. The space within the hills is in places crowded with stone huts, while, where huts do not now stand, the area is a rubbish heap of ruins where dwellings have fallen, and undoubtedly Assodé at one time was a place of considerable importance.

Among the ruins I found the ancient mosque of Assodé, the existence of which is known to every Tuareg in Aïr, and no doubt it holds a prominent place in Mohammedan religious history. The mosque stands, without any notable prominence, except in ground area, on the crown of a rising knoll in the eastern quarter of the village, with the front and tower ruins facing the north-west; possibly so that the main body of the prayer court and devotion cells face eastward toward the rising sun. The mosque is altogether in a sad state of ruin: roofs in places collapsed, lintels and door jambs fallen, and the tower (apparently never built to any great height) but a pile of fallen stones. Roughly, the mosque has a ground area of 135 ft. length and 55 ft. breadth, which longitudinally is divided into two equal sections: an indoor place of prayer and an outdoor place of prayer. The indoor section, which is the eastern half, is made up of five long dark passage-like aisles, varying from 5 ft. to 6 ft. wide, with stone walls, about 2 ft. thick, which are honeycombed with low door openings 4 ft. high, while the ceilings are only 7 ft. to 8 ft. high, constructed with timbers carrying an earth and gravel roof. The outdoor section is simply an open courtyard, surrounded by a stone wall and levelled off a few steps above the ground level outside. On the west of this there is a wing, 21 ft. by 78 ft., on a lower level containing a double row of aisles: possibly a special department for the devotions of priests. I found in the aisles great piles of Mohammedan literature, most beautifully penned, and regretted I could not bear it away with me so that it might be searched for ancient records relating to the history of the land. (Later I informed the French authorities of this literature, and it is possible that an effort will be made to have it brought back and preserved and thoroughly examined.)

There are monastic quarters well apart from the mosque and farther east, and they still have outline which shows that they were more extensive than any of the hut dwellings at present standing, which are small, square, single-room affairs.

All the ancient huts of the age of the mosque are completely in ruins and but piles of building stones, so that one cannot judge the shape which they possessed, but it is highly probable that they were of the same style as those at present standing.

There are no date palms at Assodé, but numerous signs that the inhabitants kept goats and camels.

19th June.—We left Assodé an hour and a half before daylight, and, on account of the chapter of incidents about to be related, travelled without halt till 5 p.m.

Leaving Assodé, we headed south-east up the Agoras river, until we intersected our outward route to Iferouan at the point where we had camped ten days before at the junction of the Teguednu and Asselar rivers, at which time the large conspicuous mountain named Goundai, which I remarked on when outward bound, was again in view.

It was at this point that tremendous excitement was suddenly aroused among the goumiers in finding fresh tracks of camels in the sand of the river-bed of robbers, who, coming from the north-east, had cut into our outward tracks and had gone southward following them.

High exclamations and intense excitement was rife among the goumiers for some minutes, while rifles were unslung and locks looked to and magazines fully charged, the while the tracks in the sand were being examined and read. There were, the goumiers decided, twelve camels, and their riders were undoubtedly robbers, but they were in considerable doubt as to whether they had come from Tibesti or the Ahaggar mountains, and such signs as they picked up—an end of cord, a small piece of cotton garb, and a few dried dates; articles all eagerly examined—failed to prove conclusively whether the band were Tébu or Hogar natives.

I had intended to camp at Tiggeur for the day, but now decided to rapidly follow the tracks of the robbers in the hope of arriving in time to aid the natives of Timia, if aid were needed. So we hurried on, following the course of a deep ravine; and all the time the tracks in the sand were being keenly read by the excited goumiers. In time, some miles from Timia, we came to where the robbers had happened on a herd of goats tended by a woman. Here it was noted in the sand that they had spurred their camels to rush forward so that they might catch and seize the woman, and signs of struggle were found below an acacia tree, where they had effected her capture. Thereafter they had driven the goats before them along the ravine until a side-branch was reached, and we traced where one man had turned up this on foot and gone off eastward with the captured herd, while the main band had continued in towards Timia, led by the woman they had taken prisoner, and whose sandal-prints could be traced in the sand. (It was presumed that the goats would be driven to some rendezvous where the band would meet later; but this proved wrong conjecture, for it was afterwards found that they had abandoned the goats.) Again, farther on, we traced in the sand where all the robbers had dismounted and advanced stealthily to where some donkeys were grazing; no doubt with the purpose of catching anyone who might be in attendance so that he or she would not escape to give the alarm in Timia. But there was no sign of an additional prisoner having been taken, and the robbers had continued onward, taking the donkeys with them for a short distance, and then had turned them aside up a quiet gulley and left them there.

At last, having left the ravine to ascend over a stony stretch of land and then descend into Timia valley, we came upon the place—just before the river bends toward the village, and in shelter of a jutting hill-spur—where, in the dusk, the robbers had made camp. They had lain beside their camels and reposed, and had apparently partaken of little food beyond dried dates, as they had not dared to light fires. From this camping-place, where they waited the advent of dawn, we traced the naked footprints of two of the robbers who, in the dark, had crept stealthily in to Timia to reconnoitre.

In a few minutes more we were on the outskirts of Timia, which seemed strangely deserted and silent. However, we soon espied a single armed man dodging about in a date grove, and hailed him that we were friends, whereupon he and two others came out to join us, and soon the hurried tale of the adventures of the day was being poured into the ears of my excited goumiers.

To begin with: we were too late! Timia had been attacked and entered, and the robbers had left, heading south, about four hours ago. The disjointed story of the natives pieced together something in this form: The robbers had attacked Timia at dawn to-day, trying to terrorise the place. But the inhabitants had had warning the evening before, brought in by a woman, who had been with the donkeys, which the robbers had come across, and who had fled undetected some little time before the bandits had reached the animals. So that the Timia natives (who were unfortunately without the leadership of their chief Fougda: reputed to be an able man in circumstances of danger) were already secreted among the rocks in the gorge at dawn awaiting the robbers. Also they had wisely sent a man to where their camels were grazing south-west of Timia, with instructions that they were to be driven with all haste on to the Baguezan plateau (an order which events proved was not explicitly obeyed). Therefore, when the robbers advanced, they found the natives waiting for them, and, apparently, regular guerilla warfare ensued which lasted for some hours. It would appear that the Timia natives were foolish, and blazed off their ammunition at ineffective range; for, apparently, they did not hit a single robber, while they completely exhausted their scant supplies of ammunition. On the other hand the robbers were very daring and wily in attack and better marksmen, also they had modern rifles and plenty of ammunition (later I picked up a full clasp—6 rounds— of ·303 Italian ammunition and some empty cases of Turkish ammunition of about ·44 calibre).

About noon the village was completely at the mercy of the robbers, and they entered where they willed. But, be it said to their credit, they made no attempt to wreak vengeance on the people or their dwellings, and they carried off neither quantities of food nor goats nor women. Their sole purpose was to steal camels, and as none were in the village or near by, they forthwith forced the old headman, whom they had captured, to guide them out of the village and take them to where the camels were to be found.

This was as far as their story went. At the time we arrived in Timia the robbers were somewhere to the south, searching for the camels belonging to the natives.

I was in a quandary, for I felt sure the robbers could yet be caught, yet if I led the goumiers against the robbers without real personal cause and failed to rout them, or suffered heavy casualties, I might be asked awkward questions by the French authorities and be asked to leave the country; which would be disastrous to the interests of the expedition. Therefore, after due consideration of my position as a civilian in a foreign land, which barred me from pursuing the enemy with no other purpose than to force a fight, I called the chief goumier and Atagoom, and told them that I was certain that if their captain at Agades knew they were close to robbers, he would expect them to follow them up, while, if they did not, he would be sure to be vastly displeased—this was, I felt, as far as I could go in the matter. And my reasoning bore fruit, for the goumiers agreed to follow the robbers, reinforced by five armed natives of Timia, and though both men and beasts were terribly tired, having travelled since 4.30 in the morning, they set out to follow the tracks of the robbers just as it was growing dusk.

As soon as I had got them away, I sent the half-dozen unarmed men remaining in Timia to look for wounded, and before retiring to rest dressed, as best I could, with warm water and bandages, three bad cases which they brought in: one of whom I did not expect to live.

The old headman wearily returned to Timia at night, leaning heavily on his staff and barely able to walk, for, besides his trying experiences in the hands of the robbers, he was slightly wounded in the chin and right knee. The robbers had released him when they had sighted the camels they sought. He said the robbers were Hogar, and the band comprised twelve camels (as the goumiers had accurately read from the mingled tracks in the sand), fourteen men, and thirteen rifles. (Those robbers sometimes mount two men on one camel.)

Timia, 20th June.—Spent an uneventful night alone: no further disturbance.

This morning a few natives begin to appear out of hiding and come to my camping-place to express their gladness that I have returned to protect them. (For they have great faith in the powers of any white man.) They are still in a state of panic, and most of the women and children remain hidden among the rocks in the mountain sides afraid to come in, especially as they fear a second band which the robbers declared would follow them in a day or two; a declaration which proved without truth, and circulated by the robbers solely to intimidate the populace and prevent the men of Timia from leaving the neighbourhood to follow them. For my own part I remain camped in the open by the edge of the dry river-bed, in spite of remonstrance from the old headman, who wanted me also to hide in the hills; and before the end of the day my apparent indifference had helped to restore native confidence.

During the day five more wounded were brought in to be attended to, in addition to the three placed in my charge last evening: one of whom had died during the night.

The goumiers returned late to-night, reporting they had not caught up the robbers, who had succeeded in capturing (about midway between Timia and Baguezan plateau) and driving off thirty-two camels. The native guarding the camels, who had unfortunately dallied in executing the order to drive the camels rapidly away into Baguezan, had been caught by the robbers and disrobed of everything he possessed except a leather loincloth.

21st June.—I now proposed to remain and collect at Timia for some time; therefore, as arranged, I sent off news to Agades of my safe return from northern Aïr, at the same time returning all the goumiers, excepting the two worthies Atagoom and Saidi.

Two of my patients passed away overnight, both with very bad internal wounds. Three have now succumbed to wounds out of the eight brought in. The remainder are all likely to recover.

22nd June.—Quiet day skinning, and Timia now rapidly returning to a normal state. This morning witnessed the arrival of many of the fugitive population from hiding in the mountains. They came in twos or threes and small parties: some men, with staves and bundles on their shoulders; but mostly women, liberally clad, for warmth at night, in cotton clothing, and carrying rolled-up grass mats upon which they had slept among the rocks. Some of the women also drove in goats before them.

Further information with regard to the robbers was revealed to me to-day by the old headman, who is now recovering from his wounds. It appears that on the way to Timia the robbers came upon and caught one of the "wild" women from Tamgak mountain which we had run across north of Egouloulof, and had questioned her closely as to whom it was who had passed northward and left behind the many camel tracks. She informed them there was a white man and many armed natives, who had gone to Iferouan; whereupon they showed signs of uneasiness, and threw the woman aside, while exclaiming denunciations on our heads, and, among themselves, saying that they must now hasten on their way to Timia, lest we return on their heels or intercept them on their way north.

It is also now known definitely that the robber band were Hogar natives, and came from Janet, a short distance south-west of Ghat, in the territory of the Asger (Asdjer, Azkar), approximately some 500 miles north of Timia, and were led by a famous and much-feared robber chief named Chebickee. The old headman, who, of course, had ample opportunity to see everything while captive, says the band were mounted on exceptionally fine camels, as I and the goumiers had already surmised from the large footprints in the sand.

I remained on in Timia while the wounded recovered and the little village among the mountains gradually settled down to wonted peacefulness.

CHAPTER XIV
EAST OF BAGUEZAN, AOUDERAS, AND TARROUAJI

AFTER collecting specimens for some little time in the pleasant neighbourhood of Timia, I set out to return to my base camp on Baguezan, not by the route I had come, but round by the east side of the mountain, via Tebernit valley, and thereafter along the southern base until we should come to the pass above Tokede which I had originally climbed. There is no pass in the northern or eastern mountain-sides of Baguezan.

The journey by this route occupied four days, as against two and a half days by the more direct route on the western side by which I had travelled outward to Timia. But, in general, the east side of Baguezan is easier to travel along with camels than the rugged western side, for there it is possible to skirt the margin of the stony foothills that lie out from the base and travel along the edge of the sand or over fairly level gravel-covered ground.

The eastern aspect of Baguezan Mountains differs from that of the west in that it presents a more abrupt mountain face and has less bulwark of rugged foothills than in the west, where the whole country below the plateau is broken and mountainous; while out beyond the foothill margin on the east side, east of the shallow Tebernit valley, the land stretches away in a flat-looking plain, which contains very few detached hills, and, in places, bears a fair growth of open acacia bush.

Leaving Tebernit valley and advancing round the south-east

corner of Baguezan the Ouna and Nabaro rivers are crossed: wide dry stream-beds rising from deep crevices in the mountain-side. There are some particularly large acacias growing on the banks of the Ouna river, while there is a deserted village on the south bank of the stream. Altitude, a short distance north of Ouna river, 3,300 ft.

So completely deserted is Ouna village and the whole territory, that I see, as I have seen elsewhere, confident gazelles resting in the street spaces, while their footprints mark the sand even to the very doors of the dwellings.

Dorcas Gazelles are fairly plentiful in the country east of Baguezan, and there are also a few Dama Gazelles, while there are Wild Sheep on the mountain faces; but, so far as the latter are concerned, the rugged western side of the mountain is much the better hunting-ground.

The flatness of the country east of Baguezan continues round into the south-east for a long way, and it is not until Adekakit river is reached that the aspect changes and one begins to enter rugged foothills.

Adekakit river, which rises in a remarkably deep ravine on the mountain face, is a broad river-bed, with fairly fertile banks, which support some dum palms, and the south side of the mountain appears to be the only locality around Baguezan base where those trees grow.

By the time Teouar is reached, one has entered a land of mountain foothill environment and encounters many scenes of rugged beauty. Particularly fine in that respect is the journey up the Tessouma river-bed from Teouar to Tokede. The stream-bed is here very broad, and well garbed with trees on either bank, dum palm, a few date palms, acacia and "Abisgee" bush, while its course is channelled, latterly in a deep twisting rock-banked gorge, through a land of mountains, some of which have such grotesque shapes and towering heights that they command acute admiration and attention.

Teouar village (altitude, 3,050 ft.) stands on high stony ground on the east bank of the river. It is a deserted village of stone huts. Across the river there are some date palms, and here we found two natives cultivating the ground beneath the palms in spite of their constant fear of robbers. So great is their dread, that at our approach to Teouar we descried two figures fleeing into the hills until I sent the goumiers in chase of them, and to hail them that we were friends. One was armed with a huge heavy long-barrelled rifle, long out of date, while the other had only a hand-spear.

I have already described the ascent from Tokede to Baguezan plateau, so that the final stage of my journey back into Baguezan need not here be dwelt on.

It was early in July when I re-entered Baguezan, and I was astonished and delighted at the change which, owing to considerable rain showers in June, had taken place during my absence. Where all had been bleak and overshadowed with the melancholy grey of bare rocky hills, there are now valleys bearing green-leafed trees and green grass, while even among the rocks there is a faint tint of greenness where thin grass or small plant or tiny bush has precarious lodgment. But I note no bright display of flowers, which is because the few flowering bushes and plants have blooms that are small and modest, and are hidden at any distance by the fullness of growth of green leaf and grass blade. Butterflies, hitherto remarkably scarce, are now numerous on Baguezan on account of the prevailing spring-like conditions, but they are not of great variety of kind, nor brilliantly coloured, nor large of size, being chiefly of desert forms.

The few days I remained on Baguezan were occupied, when not collecting, in packing away boxes of specimens in readiness to travel, and in mending my bush-clothes which were now in a sad state of raggedness.

On 4th July I left Baguezan mountains and set out to Agades, having, by camel courier, received a request to come in to meet the commandant of the Territoire Militaire du Niger, who was to arrive at Agades from Zinder in a few days in the course of a round of inspection of outlying posts.

I journeyed back to Agades by the way I had come, and spent three very enjoyable days at the Fort in the society of fellow Europeans—a great treat when one has been long alone except for native following.

In connection with the last remark, being *alone* on work of this kind has, I have concluded, one advantage, which may be set against its harshness in denying companionship; and that is the rare opportunity which it gives to undistracted study. When a man in ordinary business life wishes to pursue deep study, it is common habit to select a quiet room where he may sit alone in undisturbed contemplation of his subject. And a similar privacy has, I believe, its advantages to the man out on the trail: alone, he is better equipped to give undivided attention to study, so long as the period of research is not too protracted and the strain of loneliness not unbearable to the point of depression. But besides this advantage to study, besides the fate which circumstances may impose, I would be one of the first to say to anyone contemplating a journey beyond civilised frontiers: "Never go without a well-tried comrade—if you can help it."

TEOUAR, A TYPICAL DESERTED VILLAGE OF AÏR.

But to return to my narrative. On the way in to Agades I experienced a rain-storm, which illustrates how local such occurrences often are. My caravan was five miles north-east of Agades on the evening of 7th July, when we saw black threatening clouds rolling in the distance apparently over Agades, and, judging it prudent not to run into the storm, we camped at Azzal for the night. At Azzal we experienced strong wind and a very light shower, but on entering Agades next morning we learned that on the previous evening a regular tornado had descended upon the place (which wrecked the wireless plant) and torrential rains had fallen. The after result will be that at Agades (without rain until this storm) the vegetation will now rapidly grow fresh and green, while Azzal and the other places unwatered will remain dormant. Hence at this season parts of Aïr may be green, like Baguezan and localities further north, and others parched and leafless.

It was during this journey to Agades that some particularly fine deceptive mirages were seen. At times lakes of blue water bordered with marsh would be apparent away in the distance, always, of course, to fade out long before the traveller could draw near to the alluring picture. The whole illusion is perfectly clear to the healthy traveller, but what a thing of torture such picture could be to any unfortunate man in search of water in the barren land—lakes lying before our eyes, but for ever receding out of agonised reach.

After my brief visit to Agades, which had interrupted previous plans, I turned again northward, with the purpose of travelling to Aouderas, where I had originally intended to go direct from Baguezan.

On the way north I camped at Azzal (altitude, 1,825 ft.) for a week to make some collections, and, in particular, to capture some specimens of the beautiful Bee-eater, *Merops albicollis albicollis*, which up to that time I had not seen elsewhere.

It was here, at the settlement on the banks of the Azzal river, which contains many of the natives evacuated from northern Aïr, that I found the Chief of Iferouan with a number of his tribe about him. His people had been accustomed to grow wheat at Iferouan, and it was interesting to note that they had commenced, with considerable success, to establish the same crop cultivation at Azzal, with the aid of deep wells and primitive irrigation. But the Chief declared that he and his people longed to be free to return to Iferouan— "Our hearts are there, not in Azzal." A sentiment which recalled the words of the Chief of Baguezan in decrying the Sahara south of Aïr as of no attraction to his people: "There are no mountains there, and how could we live without them!"

The Chief of Iferouan had been across Africa on the old pilgrim route, which he described to me as follows: From the country of the Tuaregs in the neighbourhood of Timbuktu the route crosses Upper Senegal to Zinder on the Niger river, thence it skirts the northern borders of Sokoto (Nigeria), and then strikes north-east to Agades, and continues through Aïr via Aouderas, Aguellal, and Iferouan (or alternatively via Assodé), thereafter continuing away northward to Tripoli on the seaboard of the Mediterranean, touching on the way the important points of Ghat, Rhadames, and Djebel. So far as this ancient pilgrim route concerns Aïr, the old caravan roads are still to be seen with undiminished clearness when they pass over stony ground where no sand accumulates and not a blade of vegetation has root. At such places one may see ten to fifteen single foot-wide paths running parallel to each other camel-width apart, light-coloured clearly defined lines where the dark gravel surface of the natural ground has been brushed aside or powdered down by passage of countless feet. When those old roads lead off such stony ground through rocks between hills or over ridges, where the way is barred with rocks and boulders, the road changes always to a narrow much-worn single defile, which turns and twists where passage for camels has been found possible, or, by labour of hands, made possible. Again, when those old roads enter and continue along the loose sandy bed of a dry river, there remains no sign of track whatever, as all marks have been long washed away by wind and flood.

Accompanied by ten goumiers, I left Azzal on the 19th July *en route* to Aouderas, three days' journey north. At Dabaga, on the Azzal river, we branched off the route to Baguezan, and headed due north until we cut into the Tilisdak river, when we turned eastward until Aouderas was reached. I will not enter upon detailed description of the journey to Aouderas, for the barren country was of the same rugged, stony, hill-dotted nature as that described south of Baguezan. The altitude at Dabaga registered 2,100 ft., at Germat, on the Tilisdak river, 2,350 ft., and at Aouderas, 2,700 ft., so that (as experienced on the journey to Baguezan) a decided ascent takes place between Agades (1,710 ft.) and the base of the most southern mountain ranges, once the sand plains are left behind and the true rock region of Aïr entered.

Fortunately it was not a very long journey to Aouderas, for the climate at this time was particularly trying, as it was the season preceding the Rains, which period, and the period just after the Rains, are the most unhealthy for European or native, and much sickness (principally malaria) then prevails. At these times many of the days are unpleasantly hot and enervating— days that from sunrise to sunset are breathless and sultry and heavily oppressive. While, as to the intensity of the heat, an afternoon temperature on 20th July registered 102° Fahr. in the shade.

The little village of Aouderas is tucked away in an open glen in the foothills of Aouderas mountains, and is surrounded on all sides by rugged hills and mountainous landscape. The Aouderas river runs through the glen, and the village is built upon its banks. In places where there are small pockets of level ground between the river-bank and the rising hill-side, there are a goodly number of date palms growing in the gardens of grain cultivated beneath their shade, which makes very attractive scenes after the barren greyness of the land to the south.

I was warmly received by the Chief of Aouderas and his tribe, who had news that I was coming, and, to my surprise, I found, as on no other like occasion, that a hut had already been built for me on a nicely cleared space of ground. I find that all Aïr natives know of "the Hunting White Man" now, and each new place that I visit, where there are natives, my welcome increases in cordiality and there is less suspicion of the stranger.

On the day I entered Aouderas there was a caravan of natives, with camels and donkeys, camped there, who, with a posse of goumiers, were, in obedience to orders from Agades, on their way north to Iferouan to gather dates, which are now ripening. Some of those natives openly declared that they were afraid of the journey, and related to me the following story: "Last year, at this season, a party went north on the same errand, and, in the night, when camped at Iberkom, they were surprised by Tébu robbers, and three of them were killed and two captured and bound and carried off, as were also all the donkeys which were to have transported the dates to Agades."

During the time I camped at Aouderas I spent much time in the mountains and witnessed many of the wild magnificent scenes which are to be found on the tops and in rock-girt valleys, whether one travels eastward or westward or northward among the many ranges. In the detached Amattasa mountains, west of Aouderas, I hunted to an altitude of 4,000 ft., which is near to but not the highest summit; and in the Aouderas mountains, north of the village, I reached an altitude over 3,000 ft., which, however, is a long way from the summit of this massive rugged range. There is some very fine scenery in the Amattasa range, while on the east side of it there is a rocky river-bed which has a course in a cliff-banked gully that cuts deeply below the level of the surrounding land. The natives call this river the Tarare. Immediately below a ruined village of the same name there is, in this stream, a remarkable dry waterfall of great height, while in deep cavities in the rock at the bottom there are pools of open water and some green vegetation; the only place in Aïr where I have found a river containing open water in the dry season which was long-lying and not the outcome of recent rains. The cliffs of the fall and the sheer banks on either side were the haunts of numerous dark-coloured apes, which stared curiously upon the strange intruders and barked repeatedly. There is, also, a cave at the foot of the east bank which the Chief of Aouderas declares used to be the home of lions.

Passing north of Amattasa mountains, the river Tarare runs out into a very wide valley of dark gravel ground, with hills and mountains on all sides; and this is the way through from Aouderas Glen to the Assada valley, which lies between Baguezan and Béla mountains, and which I had viewed, further north, from the head of the north-west pass out of Baguezan.

The Chief of Aouderas, whose name is Ochullu, proved to be a fine hunter, and thoroughly friendly, and together we hunted in all directions, sleeping among the mountains at night on occasions, so that we might travel farther and be high in the hills at break of day.

Besides collecting birds, and small mammals, and butterflies in the Aouderas neighbourhood, I had the good fortune to kill three wild sheep (wily difficult animals to approach), one of them a nice museum specimen, which was skinned complete, while another proved to be the largest of the kind which I shot in Aïr, weighing 164 lbs., but was, unfortunately, no use as a specimen, as it had one massive horn diseased at the base.

Ochullu was not nearly so active among the rocks as Minerou (the Chief of Baguezan), and whereas Minerou had led me many a pretty dance among wild mountain-tops, I found it was now my turn to reverse the position and give Ochullu some gruelling experiences.

With reference to this subject I received about this time a letter from the Commanding Officer at Agades, which contained the following paragraph: "Minerou has come to Agades; he told me you are not fat, you climb the rocks like the Ragin-douchi (wild sheep), and you are very fond of rats; so everything is right." Let me hasten to add that even although I may be lean, I do not eat rats. (The amusing remark of Minerou is intended to refer to my efforts to collect small rodents of all kinds.)

But, to return to the subject of the preceding paragraph, if not a hard hunter, Ochullu was a wise one, who knew every crevice in the mountains and the habits of our quarry, so that it was a pleasure to set out with him.

Ochullu has a memorable mark upon his person, which I shall always associate with this "Child of the mountains"—a deep sword wound slashed across his left side, which was often exposed when he lifted his arm and the loose mantle drapings of his sleeve uncovered his swarthy side, which, below the armpit, was bare to the waist.

Ochullu, like all Tuaregs, is familiar with robbers and with fighting. In fact I believe he is inclined to be a bit of an independent outlaw himself, for he showed me a hiding-place, high in the Aouderas range, where he and his tribe had fled from the French soldiers during the 1916 rising, and where they had hidden till a peaceable truce was arranged. While now, at the time of my visit, he does not appear altogether content to acknowledge the authority of the newly appointed Sultan of Agades.

Among other interesting things, Ochullu showed me where last year, one afternoon, twelve robbers had come in close to Aouderas and lain in hiding in a ravine while two of their band went right in to the village outskirts and spoke as friends to a native woman, gathering wood, whom they craftily questioned as to the inmates of the village. They sought to obtain news of the movements of the white men in Agades; whether there were any soldiers in the neighbourhood, whether or not the Chief of Aouderas was at home in the village, and how many rifles the natives possessed. However, Ochullu and some armed men chanced to be at home at the time, which circumstance was apparently disquieting to the robbers, for they thereafter prudently withdrew, taking with them two camels which they had found grazing near where they lay in hiding. But that same band proceeded to Baguezan, and it was they who a few days later raided camels of Baguezan and killed the late Chief Yofa, as I have previously related.

Ochullu made some interesting remarks with regard to Rains. Thus far it has been a rainless year at Aouderas, like last year, and Ochullu declares that if rain does not fall with the present moon (full moon, 27th July, to-morrow), none will come this year. Further, he told me that Aouderas would still have water in the wells in the event of no proper rainfall occurring for a period of four years, while he says Iferouan, Timia, and Azzal all suffer want if there is not rainfall in two years.

Ochullu is very superstitious, and declares that if only the Sultan of Agades would call all the people of the land together and make a great united prayer to Allah, they would then surely have rain.

On 1st August I left Aouderas and started south, intending to return to Agades to commence the long journey south to Kano, after circling round the eastern side of the Massif of Tarrouaji.

Accompanied by the goumiers, I departed from Aouderas at dusk after warm leave-taking with Ochullu and many of his tribe, among whom I had been made welcome from the start; while I carried away a number of bundles of fresh dates (the first of the season), presented by the Chief in final token of goodwill: a gift which I afterwards conveyed all the way home to England. We travelled till very late by light of the full moon, and camped out in the stony Ararouat plains, which I had passed through before on the way to Baguezan.

Continuing at dawn on the following day, we crossed the extensive gravel-covered plain which lies between the Ararouat river and the northern base of Tarrouaji, and camped about noon on the In Ouajou river (altitude, 2,750 ft.), a small dry river-bed in flat country north of the massive hill range.

In the late afternoon a thunderstorm advanced over us, and, much to my relief, some rain fell; for, previous to leaving Aouderas, I had been warned that no water is to be found anywhere in the neighbourhood of Tarrouaji in the dry season, and all the goumiers were averse to my attempting to make the journey. Nevertheless, I had set out; but when search for water in the neighbourhood of our In Ouajou camp had proved completely fruitless, I began to fear that our plight would force me to give up the intention of going round Tarrouaji—and then the storm broke, leaving small pools of water in its wake, and an awkward situation was saved. As the natives put it: "Allah had listened to me."

3rd August. I remarked this morning, after the rain, a few short hours of dawn, when earth was damp and grass roots already green and the pipe of wilderness birds filled the air with unwonted cheerfulness. . . . For a moment spring in the desert . . . ere stilled in its birth by scorching sun and driving sand.

Travelled from daylight to dusk round the eastern base of Tarrouaji, and camped at a pool of water, which was found close in under the hills after some searching.

From the north and east the massif of Tarrouaji appears a great jumble of hills of no great height, which do not die out at the plain's edge with the impressive strength that may be found in great mountain slopes or towering cliffs, but rather do they tail away in broken diminishing lines to outlying plains, where little straggling hills of rock are seen as far as the eye can penetrate.

On the following day I did not resume caravan travel, but left the goumiers in camp and set out before dawn to climb into Tarrouaji hill-tops. During the day the highest of numerous altitudes recorded was 3,100 ft., and, so far as I could judge by eye, I doubt if any of the innumerable crowded hill-tops which constitute this range exceed that figure. As the altitude of our camp on the east base of the range was 2,300 ft., the actual elevation of the range itself, to its highest points, in that quarter was therefore only 800 ft.

Those hills hold wild and barren scenes and no fertility, and are seldom, if ever, entered by natives, which accounts, no doubt, for the number of Barbary Sheep which I found inhabiting this range and the ease with which I could approach them. Hitherto I had been mightily pleased if I got a single shot at sheep during a day's hunting, but on this day I killed no fewer than four animals, and looked upon half a dozen others within range which I allowed to go unharmed. It was here that I secured the best head taken by me in Aïr of the new subspecies of Barbary Sheep (*Ammotragus lervia angusi*).

5th August.—We left our camp on the east side of Tarrouaji in the middle of the night, and travelled on round to the south side of the range as far as the district known as Tin-Daouin, where we camped for the day while I skinned a specimen of vulture I had shot. Thunder had been over us yesterday, but very little rain fell; however, to-day we entered country where it was apparent there had been heavy rain yesterday, for the ground was water-soaked, and the sands of the river-beds were cast in freshly lain wavelets as the result of flood an hour or two subsided.

6th August.—We saddled our camels and were away at dawn, and travelled till 3.30 p.m., when we camped in Tin-Teborag valley (altitude, 1,900 ft.), having left the hills of Tarrouaji behind and advanced near to Agades, which now lay due west not far distant. Throughout the day the country was rolling and somewhat roughly broken, while a number of broad valleys were crossed at intervals where river tributaries trend south to join the mainstream Tin-Daouin, which passes eastward in a flat valley well away from the hills. Those valleys, with river-bed in their centre, are wide and very shallow, as is usual everywhere in lowland in Aïr, with little or no banks; merely a slight slope of gravel or rock surroundings, terminating where sand and grass tussocks and trees of the valley begin. Much of the undulating country is of pleasant warm-coloured browns and greys in certain morning and evening lights: wide stretches of ground surface of pebbles of an orderly smallness and sameness, as smoothly and well-arranged as a pebble beach on sea-shore which the tide has just left. Indeed the whole outlook in such foothill gravel country of an early morn is remarkable: strange because of the absence of earth and vegetation, but with an artistic appeal to the eye on account of its striking orderliness and cleanness and uncommon purity of colour.

On the following evening we travelled in to Agades: my travels in the mountains of Aïr at an end, and the long journey south to Nigeria all that lay between me and the completion of my travels.

CHAPTER XV
THE TUAREGS OF AÏR

Before concluding this narrative I would like to make brief reference to the native inhabitants of Aïr.

I have said elsewhere that the total population of Aïr at the present time is made up of 5,000 Tuaregs. And they are strange people—the strangest race I have ever come in contact with—independent, haughty, daring, unscrupulous, and lazy in leisure, yet fit to rank among the finest travellers and camel-riders in the world. If one is to judge these Tuaregs fairly, one must try to conceive their surroundings and realise the all-important fact that they are practically wild people in a wild land that lies remote and unknown, and that they have had no advantages to influence them to be aught but wholly primitive. While, further, it may be well to remember that they are the remnant descendants of a race that was once crafty and able in war; indeed, even in the present day, they consider themselves the aristocrats of the land, and look down with scarcely veiled contempt on all negro tribes.

To the French officers and to many Hausa natives they are known as downright rascals, because they are cunning and deceitful in the most unprincipled way the moment they have any dealings with strangers, and I imagine that among themselves they hold belief that anyone outside their own tribe is a legitimate enemy to be overcome, if possible, by cunning artifice, since strength of arms is no longer theirs.

For my own part I found the Tuaregs of Aïr difficult people to deal with, and impossible people to rely on. Except at Timia and Aouderas, I met with no sincere friendliness at their hands, and was inclined to be wholly harsh in my judgment of them all, until my later experiences prompted me to be more inclined to mitigate my opinion of their shortcomings; for, after all, especially with primitive natives, one must live among such people for a long time to break through that protective reserve that shuts out the stranger as a suspect and interloper, and to learn to know them from an intimate point of view.

In appearance these Tuaregs, who are an Arab-like Semitic race, are not tall. The men are generally of strong, wiry build, inclined, if anything, to slimness, and I have never seen one of their sex in any degree corpulent. The women are smaller than the men, many of them not much more than five feet in height, and, at middle age, often grow to moderate stoutness.

The features of the Tuareg natives are usually of a swarthy copper colour of fairly light hue, while a few of them are as yellowish-white as Arabs. Their features are, of course, not of blunt negro type, and—when they can be seen unmasked—there is a pleasant variety of facial character among them, and no two are found to be alike.

Many of the women paint their faces—especially when attending a marriage or a feast—with a hideous pigment, sometimes yellow and sometimes red.

The men, without exception, wear the *yashmak* over their faces on all occasions. This is a long swathe of cotton cloth, sometimes white, but generally dark blue or black, which is wound round the head so that the lower folds cover all the face up to the centre of the nose-bridge, while the upper folds are passed over the forehead and overlap the eyebrows, so that a hood is formed to shade the eyes from the fierce rays of the sun. All that remains visible of an individual's face are two piercing dark eyes that peer out of the narrow slit in the mask. One may know Tuaregs thus masked for months, and identify individuals by little more than their eyes; but should the *yashmak* ever be removed, the transformation is so staggering that it is impossible to recognise the person at all, since you have never seen the face before in its entirety. The women wear a cotton shawl cast over the crown of the head, in typical work-girl fashion, but they do not cover the face or wear *yashmak* in any form. Wearing the *yashmak* is a Moslem custom, but outside its religious purport I am not sure but that it is a very comfortable and sensible thing for those nomads of desert places to wear, for it serves as splendid protection to the face in biting sandstorms, since it completely covers the mouth and nostrils and ears, while it hoods the eyes from fierce and tiring sun-glare.

As to the garb of the men, they are clothed in full-flowing cotton gowns which reach almost to the ground, while folds drop from the shoulders to the elbows to look like wide sleeves without being actually sewn to that form. Underneath this robe are worn loose baggy cotton trousers secured round the waist. The robes are, in general, white or dark indigo-blue (a dye locally obtained in Hausaland, where all Tuareg clothing is bought), and the latter colour is the most becoming. All the men wear leather sandals on otherwise naked feet. For ornament they wear leather wallets containing charms and trinkets, which are hung in front of the person suspended from a cord round the neck. Bangles above the elbows on the arms are also commonly worn, usually made out of soft slate-like native stone, which may be hewn to bangle-shape and then polished to a glossy blackness;

sometimes the bangles are of cheap metal, welded out of scraps of brass or tin by the local blacksmith. All Tuaregs carry double-edged swords in a leather sheath slung over the shoulder on a strap.

TUAREG BOYS OF BAGUEZAN MOUNTAINS.

"ATAGOOM," A TUAREG NATIVE OF AÏR IN TYPICAL DRESS.

The women wear loose cotton garb swathed about them, but, being of diminutive stature, they seldom bear anything of the native gracefulness which is often associated with the men, many of whom have more than ordinary vanity as to their appearance and carry themselves accordingly. The women are much given to wearing bright coloured cottons, and sometimes the effect in sombre surroundings is very pleasant. For ornament the women principally wear bangles both on the wrists and above the elbows, necklaces to which one or more charm is attached, and earrings.

With regard to the wealth of the natives, I think it may safely be said that they are a poor people, if we except one or two chiefs who possibly have fair means. The wealthiest individual that I questioned on this matter was a native of Timia, who possessed thirty camels, which, if valued at £12 a piece—which is a fair average price—would place his total wealth at £360. But the property of the ordinary native of Aïr is usually comprised of one or two camels and a number of goats, ranging from herds of five to thirty according to their means. The camels, besides being the means of transporting private stores of grain from the south, bring in a certain ready-cash return (usually about two francs per camel per day) when hired by traders or military authorities to make up a caravan journey to Hausaland or elsewhere. The goat-herds furnish milk, which is a staple food among the Tuaregs—liquid or in the form of cheese; while male animals are butchered from time to time, the meat eaten, and the hides turned to domestic use or sold.

The Tuaregs of Aïr appear to be a fairly healthy race, but the women do not bear large families, and I am told that there is a good deal of inbreeding wherever there are small local settlements. Outside of Agades there is no European doctor (at Agades there is a doctor, the only one north of Zinder), and the country would benefit greatly if it could support an adequate medical staff.

The language of the Tuaregs, which they call Tamāshack (Temashight and Tarkiye: *Barth*), is much more difficult to learn than Hausa, and is spoken in a peculiar rapid-running fashion, which makes it very difficult to grasp the distinct sounding of the vowels. Tuareg voices are often pleasantly soft and musical.

I have remarked with interest that tree names and the names of birds and animals are well-known to almost all the natives, even boys at an early age having much knowledge of the nature about them. How many of us at home can name all the trees and birds of the common roadside? But then we are really an indoor, over-civilised people, while those natives of the outdoors *must* know Nature and something of her secrets, since she provides their livelihood: food, building material, ropes, saddlery, leather, clothing, dyes, medicines, even luxuries—all that is essential to man's needs, the Tuareg harvests from his countryside, in small portion, whether he seek among the branch-tops, or digs at the tree-roots, or kills with arrow or noose-trap, or sows and reaps grain with the two hands Creation gave him and little else besides the scraps of metal he fashions to bring to his aid.

On the other hand, so far as one can observe, these natives do not discern beauty in the scenes about them, and I have often witnessed them pass by some exceptionally fair picture without paying the slightest attention to it. They are, however, attracted by strange shapes, such as are often to be seen among the rugged mountain-tops, and they sometimes exclaim and point these out.

These natives have also some meagre knowledge of the great world outside their own land: no doubt scraps of information brought to their ears by their Mohammedan priests, or by those who have made the pilgrimage to Mecca and returned alive. They know, for instance, that there are such races as Japanese and Indians; while they have a Tamāshack name for *fish*, and know that this is a creature that lives in the water and is good to eat, though none exist anywhere in Aïr.

The Mohammedan religion, and sects of Mohammedanism, such as Senussi, constitute the faith of the natives of Aïr, and they are very devout.

In their domestic life, it seems to me, the Tuaregs know little of the beauty of love. Marriage to them is something of an animal instinct, and the devotion of the men is never sacred to one woman, for they have usually from two to four wives. As an instance of their apparent lack of deep devotion, I have seen Tuaregs, after being away on a journey with their camels for months, return to their home-village and alight on the outskirts to enter into promiscuous conversation with the crowd of men that quickly gather to hear the news the travellers bring, and have known them to spend hours thus engaged before they give a thought to go forward to their huts to greet their wives and children: surely a strange indifference to domestic devotion on the part of men who have been long away from home.

In daily life it is the custom of the natives to rise before daylight, and they are already started on the road if they are travelling, or at work about their hut doors if they are in camp, before dawn lightens the eastern horizon. But you are not to conclude from this that they are energetic people, far from it; I believe that, except when travelling, the men are the laziest people I have ever met. By 8 a.m. I have known men to lie down in their huts, and not again make any attempt to rise and exert themselves until 4 or 5 p.m. in the cool of the evening. The dreadfully hot climate tends towards such laziness, but without doubt it is inherent in the blood. And their lazy life begins in childhood, for at an early age the children are sent out by their parents to herd the goats; and through the heat of a long day the youngsters chiefly spend their time sleeping or idling beneath the shade of acacias while the animals wander at no great range. In the cool of the evening the herd-boys wake to exertion, and if flocks have strayed while unattended, they have merely to follow their footprints in the tell-tale sand to come up with them and drive them home to the village.

It is pleasant to be near a native village at sundown: to hear the clear voice of some woman who sets out along a bypath uttering some strange peculiar call known only to her herd, who will in time bleat an answer; then, so that they may be milked and sheltered for the night from prowling, destructive jackals, to see her humour them slowly homeward, repeating her call the while, as the active animals run from bush to bush in haste to ferret out a few last mouthfuls of supper; while shadows of evening deepen and the comfort of coolness sets men and women rejoicing in the village. Then may be heard, above the talk and laughter of the villagers, the thud! thud! thud! of pestle poles as women crush grain for the evening meal in wooden mortar-bowls, and the cries of nursling livestock that await their feeding-time— the bleat of suckling goats and the unhappy roaring call of the milk-hungry, impatient camel-calves.

It is the women who work: they who carry water, tend the beasts, collect firewood, prepare the evening meal; and, besides their many domestic tasks, to them also is credit due for teaching their children all that they know of home-work and bush-work, of school-learning and legend, of folksong and dance.

I would say of the Tuareg men that they are adventurers of the road; seen at a disadvantage in their villages, but active and able when away with their caravans—superb camel-riders, observant trackers, and endowed with that marvellous second sense of direction which belongs only to natives.

CHAPTER XVI
HEADING FOR HOME

Who of us who have lived in Out of the World places do not know the boundless pleasure that is ours in those memorable hours when trammels are cast aside and, task-free and care-free, we are at liberty to set out Homeward Bound! on that dream-journey that has ever been treasured as something finer than gold and oft our solace in the bitterest hours of solitude! And, at Agades, while packing up and preparing to go south, I confess to spending days of exultation, while honest John went about with a perpetual smile on his face: for he too was at last going home!

I left Agades, *en route* to the south, on 10th August, with a caravan of camels bearing boxes and bales containing my complete collections.

We had no sooner departed than we experienced terrible weather: sandstorms succeeded by thunderstorms and rain, which for the next six days caused me considerable anxiety in my efforts to protect the precious cases of specimens from damage.

On the second day we camped below Tegguidi cliff in a regular land of flood, while thunderstorm raged and rain swept down upon us in torrents, and we spent a miserable night, standing ankle-deep in water, unable to lie down on the ground to sleep.

Next day we were in the centre of lakes of water, and it was impossible for the caravan-camels to travel; indeed, it was not until late morning on the following day that the water subsided sufficiently to permit of foothold for the camels and we were able to load up and, with difficulty, get out of the predicament.

The advent of Rains had set the game moving northward out of the bush-country, and, when travelling between Tegguidi and Abellama, great numbers were seen out on open plains which had been bleak and barren sand-wastes when I had passed northward, but which now contained patches of fresh grass-greenness. Dama Gazelles (*Gazella dama damergouensis*, subsp. nov.: Hausa: Mena) were most numerous, and many large herds of them were seen, and I counted herds of 37, 44, and 84. Dorcas Gazelles (*Gazella dorcas dorcas*: Hausa: Matakundi) were also plentiful, while I also saw a few handsome White Oryx (*Oryx algazel algazel*).

A day later Egyptian kites and marabou, and black and white storks were very common feeding on the abundance of locusts which now infested the green vegetation, the former catching locusts on the wing or swooping to pick them off grass-blades with their well-known dexterity. None of these birds had been present in this locality in the dry season.

On 16th August I reached the lonely post of Aderbissinat, and camped there for two weeks while collecting waterfowl and hunting again for ostrich. Much water had collected in ponds in Aderbissinat valley, and here, and henceforth, territory that had appeared bleak and barren when I passed northward was now green and fresh and well-watered, and completely changed in aspect. Waterfowl were unknown in the territory in the dry season, but now I found them plentiful: geese, ducks, waders; even gulls. But the advent of rain had brought one evil upon

Aderbissinat—it was infested with mosquitoes, and much malaria was prevalent among the native soldiers of the Fort.

AGADES FORT, BUILT WITH CLAY-MUD.

CAUGHT IN FLOOD RAINS BELOW TEGGUIDI.

Aderbissinat, as I have already stated, is on the southern borders of Aïr, and in departing from it on 30th August I bid final farewell to the strange land I had come so far to explore.

In pursuit of my zoological research I calculate my camel-caravan travelled the following distances in Aïr:

	Miles
Aderbissinat to Agades	93½
Agades to Tasessat, Baguezan Mountains	79
Tasessat to Timia	49
Timia to Iferouan	77
Iferouan to Aguellal	31
Aguellal to Assodé	40
Assodé to Timia	30
Timia to Tasessat via east side of Baguezan	73
Tasessat to Agades	79
Agades to Aouderas via Tilisdak river	62
Aouderas to Agades via east side of Tarrouaji	93
Agades to Aderbissinat	93½
Total caravan travel in Aïr	800
Kano to Aderbissinat	303
Aderbissinat to Kano	303
Total travel with camels	1,406

There is one point I would like to refer to before departing from the subject of Aïr. Aïr has been termed in the past on African maps and in textbooks a great "oasis," a word which I take it means a "fertile place in a sandy desert"; a concise enough explanation, unless one endows it with a wider, less clearly defined latitude. But it appears to me that such a term applied to Aïr, inferring as it does that the country is fertile, is an imposition on the word that is apt to be misleading to anyone who endeavours to conceive, through the medium of description, the real composition of the country. And I hold this belief because during the dry season *I cannot imagine a more barren country than Aïr* in all the world: mountain after mountain of bare rock and far-reaching lowlands of nothing but dark gravel-covered ground, bleak as a ploughed field in winter time, except for scant rifts of green along shallow sandy river-beds or close under mountain slopes. Without doubt Aïr is bleak almost as the veriest desert: the one a vast lifeless scene of rock and boulder and pebble, the other great wastes of sand. For my own part, therefore, I am happier and much more sure of my ground when, in speaking of the country, I refer to it nominally as "The mountain land of Aïr," and am sure that at the present time it has no real claim to be termed an "oasis" unless in the height of a good season of rain.

From Aderbissinat I travelled south to Tanout, where I camped in the hope of securing an ostrich, as I had met with no success in hunting for those birds up till that time. Here, however, owing solely to the keenness of the French officer at the Fort, I managed to secure a very fine adult male ostrich, which proved on later examination to be the same species as is found elsewhere in Africa: *Struthio camelus camelus*. Those birds carry a large quantity of fat, and the task of skinning this specimen, and cleaning and drying the skin free of oily matter with due regard to keeping the rich plumes unsoiled, occupied no less than two days.

Tanout, like everywhere else now, was greatly changed since I had passed north, and I found all the inhabitants in the fields cultivating large areas of millet which had already sprung up almost to man-height. All natives declare it has been a bountiful and wonderful season of rain; which has fallen here earlier than farther north.

North of Tanout the country is uninhabited (except for a few roving Tuaregs) and uncultivated; but on resuming the journey south of this Fort, I thenceforth passed green fields of millet each day.

I need not dwell further on my return journey to Nigeria, via Zinder, for it was henceforth, until our destination was reached, simply routine of continual wearisome grinding travel, while I suffered from fitful attacks of malaria which I had contracted at Aderbissinat.

On 22nd September I re-entered Kano. All that I find recorded in my diary of this, to me, memorable day is: "The trail has ended—the camels have gone and faithful Dogo—and I miss the fretful roar of the beasts, and the soft speech of the Tuaregs, and the glow of the camp-fire. . . . Everyone is most kind in welcoming me safely back." But it needs no diary to recall the day of my arrival in Kano—when the long trail finished, and riding saddles and pack saddles and a band of sorely tried camels were freed upon the sand from precious loads of specimens which they had carried for many months. That great last day when work was done—the burden and worry of it all thrown to the four winds—the warm handshake of friends awaiting to welcome me in—a day, indeed, rare in a lifetime.

Yes! I was back among my own people at last, had drifted in unannounced like the sandstorms that fitfully bore me company from the north, no one knowing of my coming until a ragged figure was in the streets of the European settlement, where civilisation and railway begin and the desolation of the Sudan ends.

Fourteen hundred miles lay behind me in my camels' tracks, and all of the months of a year but one since the day I left home.

Assuredly, and perhaps I may be forgiven for thinking so, it was good to be back on British soil, good to hear my own tongue spoken, and good to look on the broad grin on John's face. "Kano is sweet past Zinder," he had said long ago, and boarding the steamer at Lagos a few days later, while honest John stood by with tears in his eyes and repeated injunctions that "master" was to hurry to return, I said to him: "Yes, John, what you mean is: 'Home is sweet past anywhere else on earth—and you are right!'" And I stepped on board, followed by John's parting cry ringing in my ears: "Sai wata rana" (Farewell till another day).

APPENDIX

NEW SPECIES AND SUBSPECIES DISCOVERED DURING THE EXPEDITION

NEW SPECIES AND SUBSPECIES OF MAMMALS (OTHER THAN RUMINANTS)

Described by Messrs. OLDFIELD THOMAS and MARTIN A. C. HINTON of the British Museum (Natural History). (The complete collection is fully described by Messrs. THOMAS and HINTON in *Novitates Zoologicæ*, the Journal of the Tring Museum, vol. xxviii., pp. 1-13, 1921.)

	Locality taken
Wild cat: *Felis haussa* sp. nov.	Kano and Damagarim.
Caracal (Lynx): *Caracal caracal poecilotis* subsp. nov.	Baguezan Mts.
Pale sand-coloured fox: *Vulpes pallida harterti* subsp. nov.	Damergou and Aïr.
Silver-grey fox: *Vulpes rüppelli cæsia* subsp. nov.	Aïr.
Striped weasel: *Poecilictis rothschildi* sp. nov.	Kano.

Ground Squirrel: *Euxerus erythropus agadius* subsp. nov.	Aïr.
Naked-soled gerbil: *Taterillus gracilis angelus* subsp. nov.	Kano.
Nigerian hairy-soled gerbil: *Gerbillus nigeriæ* sp. nov.	Kano and Damagarim.
Dwarf gerbil: *Desmodilliscus buchanani* sp. nov.	Kano.
Fat-tailed mouse: *Steatomys cuppedius* sp. nov.	Kano.
Giant rat: *Cricetomys buchanani* sp. nov.	Kano.
Dwarf mouse: *Leggada haussa* sp. nov.	Kano and Damagarim.
Spiney rock mouse: *Acomys airensis* sp. nov.	Aïr.
Striped bush mouse: *Lemniscomys olga* sp. nov.	Damergou.
Jerboa: *Jaculus jaculus airensis* subsp. nov.	Damergou and Aïr.
Gundi: *Massoutiera rothschildi* sp. nov.	Aïr.
Short-eared hare: *Lepus canopus* sp. nov.	Kano.
Rock dassie: *Procavia buchanani* sp. nov.	Aïr.

With regard to the entire collection of mammals (other than Ruminants), in which is contained the above species and subspecies which are new, the British Museum paper, in the foreword makes the following appreciative statements:

"Thanks to the kindness of Lord Rothschild we are now able to give a list of the complete collection made by Captain

Buchanan, both of such further mammals as he obtained in the Kano region and of those which he got northwards to Aïr itself, which he explored most successfully.

As this is a country which has been hitherto entirely out of the ken of mammalogists, we were prepared to expect a considerable number of new forms to be discovered, but we certainly never expected that so very high a proportion of the species would be new. Indeed we believe it may safely be said that in the history of mammalogy no collection containing so high a proportion of novelties has ever come to Europe from a continental locality.

In all, the collection contains 36 species and subspecies, of which no less than 18 are new, 6 of these latter having been described in our previous paper. Considering the comparatively barren nature of the country, and the number of mammals usually found to occur in any given area, the capture of 36 forms indicates that Captain Buchanan has been highly successful in getting a full representation of the fauna of the districts he has worked in. . . .

"As already stated, the National Museum has to thank Lord Rothschild for a full set of the mammals dealt with, including all the types. The skins are all beautifully prepared, and Captain Buchanan is to be congratulated on the great value that his collection has proved to possess."

NEW SUBSPECIES OF UNGULATE MAMMALS

Described by LORD ROTHSCHILD, F.R.S., Ph.D. (The complete collection of Ungulate Mammals is fully described by LORD ROTHSCHILD in *Novitates Zoologicæ*, the Journal of the Tring Museum, vol. xxviii., pp. 75-77, 1921.)

	Locality taken
Arui, Udad, or Barbary sheep: *Ammotragus lervia angusi* subsp. nov. (Largest head collected: right horn 21 in. over curve; left horn 20$^8/_{10}$ in.)	Aïr.
Dama gazelle: *Gazella dama damergouensis* subsp. nov. (Largest head collected: length of horns 5$^6/_{10}$ ins.)	Damergou.

NEW SUBSPECIES OF BIRDS

Described by Dr. ERNST HARTERT, Director of Tring Museum. (The complete collection of Birds is fully described by Dr. HARTERT in *Novitates Zoologicæ*, vol. xxviii., pp. 78-141, 1921.)

	Locality taken
Subsaharan striped kingfisher: *Halcyon chelicuti eremogiton* subsp. nov.	Kano and Damagarim.
Straight-billed wood-hoopoe: *Scoptelus aterrimus cryptostictus* subsp. nov.	Aïr.
Golden goatsucker: *Caprimulgus eximus simplicior* subsp. nov.	Damagarim and Damergou.
Sand martin: *Riparia obsoleta buchanani* subsp. nov.	Aïr.
Sombre rock-chat: *Cercomela melanura airensis* subsp. nov.	Aïr.

Northern ant-eating wheatear[11]: *Myrmecocichla æthiops buchanani* subsp. nov.	Kano, Damagarim, and Damergou.
Saharan bush-babbler: *Crateropus fulvus buchanani* subsp. nov.	Aïr.
Grey bush-babbler: *Crateropus plebejus anomalus* subsp. nov.	Kano.
Long-tailed sunbird: *Nectarinia pulchella ægra* subsp. nov.	Kano, Damagarim, and Aïr.
Crested shrike: *Prionops plumatus haussarum* subsp. nov.	Kano.
Asben brown pipit[11]: *Anthus sordidus asbenaicus* subsp. nov.	Aïr.
Dunn's desert lark: *"Calendula" dunni pallidor* subsp. nov.	Damergou.
Small rock sparrow: *Petronia dentata buchanani* subsp. nov.	Damagarim.
Pencil-crowned weaver-bird: *Sporopipes frontalis pallidior* subsp. nov.	Damagarim and Damergou.

Dr. Hartert, in his most interesting foreword to his paper (which deals extensively with the zoo-geographical history of the Sahara and the important information which the Expedition has brought to light in that connection), states two facts which have a particular bearing on the value of the collection of birds:

"Zoologically Aïr remained absolutely unknown until Buchanan's expedition. It was with great satisfaction to myself that Lord Rothschild fell in with my ideas about it, with his usual zeal and interest in all scientific exploration, and that Captain

Buchanan accepted the offer to make a collecting trip to Aïr for the Tring Museum. The exploration of that country has been in my mind since 1886. . . . It was one of my many unfulfilled dreams of life to visit Asben myself, but I have never given up hope one day to see natural history specimens from there. . . .

"Captain Buchanan obtained skins of 168 species. In a country which, to a great extent, is desert and therefore poor in animal life, and considering that he also collected as many Lepidoptera and mammalia as possible, this is a very fine collection."

NEW SPECIES AND SUBSPECIES OF BUTTERFLIES AND MOTHS

Described by LORD ROTHSCHILD, F.R.S., Ph.D. (The complete collection is fully described by LORD ROTHSCHILD in *Novitates Zoologicæ*.)

BUTTERFLIES

	Locality taken
Teracolus amelia f. arid. insignis f. nov.	Kano.
Teracolus celimene angusi subsp. nov.	Damagarim.
Teracolus liagore f. pluv. *liagoroides* f. nov.	Aïr.
Eronia bugueti buchanani subsp. nov.	Damergou.
Terias flavicola f. arid. parva f. nov.	Kano.
Vivachola livia pallescens subsp. nov.	Damagarim and Aïr.

Spindasis buchanani sp. nov.	Kano and Damagarim.

MOTHS

Aegocera brevivitta rectilineoides subsp. nov.	Damergou.
Timora buchanani sp. nov.	Aïr.
Timora terracottoides sp. nov.	Damagarim.
Adisura affinis sp. nov.	Damagarim.
Eublemma dissoluta sp. nov.	Damagarim.
Eublemma bipartita sp. nov.	Damergou.
Eublemma perkea sp. nov.	Damagarim.
Eublemma pseudonoctna sp. nov.	Damagarim.
Ozarba damagarima sp. nov.	Damagarim, Damergou, and Aïr.
Pseudozarba abbreviata sp. nov.	Aïr.
Pseudozarba bella sp. nov.	Aïr.
Enlocastra sahariensis sp. nov.	Damagarim.
Enlocastra pseudozarboides sp. nov.	Aïr.
Tarache buchanani sp. nov.	Damergou and Aïr.
Tarache asbenensis sp. nov.	Aïr.
Crypsotidia griseola sp. nov.	Damagarim.
Crypsotidia parva sp. nov.	Kano.
Grammodes buchanani sp. nov.	Damagarim.
Parachalciope mixta sp. nov.	Locality not noted.
Raphia buchanani sp. nov.	Kano.
Rhynchina sahariensis sp. nov.	Damagarim, Damergou, and Aïr.
Rhynchina buchanani sp. nov.	Aïr.
Hypena sordida sp. nov.	Damagarim.

Casama griseola sp. nov.	Damagarim and Damergou.
Acidaliastis micra dissimilis ab. saturata ab. nov.	Aïr.
Tephrina quadriplaga sp. nov.	Damergou.
Paropta buchanani sp. nov.	Aïr.
Anadiasa sahariensis sp. nov.	Aïr.
Pachypasa concolor sp. nov.	Aïr.
Miresa coccinea intensior subsp. nov.	Damagarim.
Ommatopteryx hampsoni sp. nov.	Aïr.
Ommatopteryx asbenicola sp. nov.	Aïr.
Surattha albostigmata sp. nov.	Aïr.
Heterographis medioalba sp. nov.	Damergou.
Heterographis airensis sp. nov.	Aïr.
Heterographis eximia sp. nov.	Aïr.
Heterographis sahariensis sp. nov.	Damagarim and Aïr.
Heterographis cretaceogrisea sp. nov.	Damagarim, Damergou, and Aïr.
Homœosoma straminea sp. nov.	Damagarim.
Homœosoma basalis sp. nov.	Aïr.
Homœosoma asbenicola sp. nov.	Aïr.
Brephia inconspicua sp. nov.	Aïr.
Brephia gracilis sp. nov.	Aïr.
Crocidomera intensifasciata sp. nov.	Aïr.
Pogononeura buchanani sp. nov.	Aïr.
Anerastia aurantiaca sp. nov.	Aïr.
Pterothrix damergouensis sp. nov.	Damergou.
Crocolia africana sp. nov.	Damergou and Aïr.

Pyralis soudanesis sp. nov.	Damagarim, Damergou, and Aïr.
Tyndis umbrosus sp. nov.	Aïr.
Bostra asbenicola sp. nov.	Aïr.
Dattima buchanani sp. nov.	Aïr.
Dattima dubiosa sp. nov.	Aïr.
Marasmia hampsoni sp. nov.	Kano.
Loxostege damergouensis sp. nov.	Damergou.
Cybolomia azzalana sp. nov.	Aïr.
Cybolomia ledereri sp. nov.	Damergou.
Cybolomia fenestrata sp. nov	Aïr.
Metasia angustipennis sp. nov.	Damagarim.
Metasia parallelalis sp. nov.	Damagarim.
Tegostoma camparalis sahariensis subsp. nov.	Damergou and Aïr.

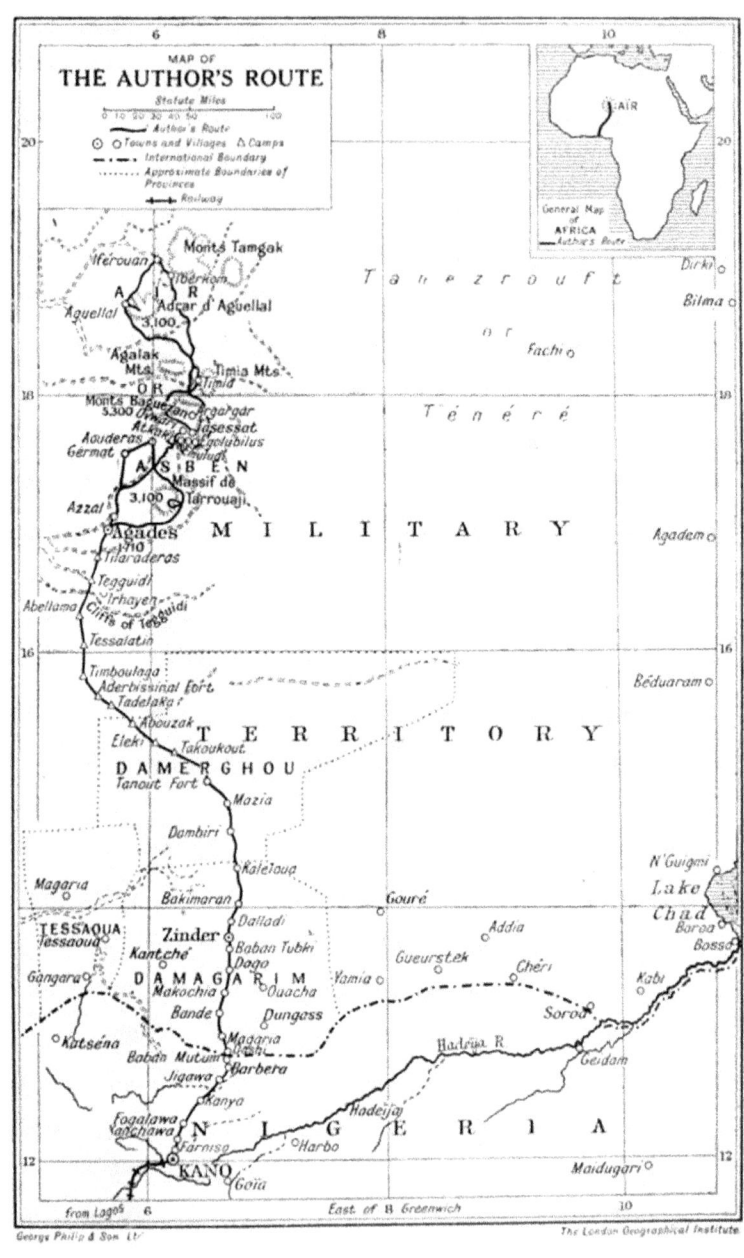

MAP OF
THE AUTHOR'S ROUTE

FOOTNOTES

[1] Director of Tring Museum.

[2] Of the British Museum of Natural History.

[3] But this he did not do, for I never saw him again.

[4] Nigeria handbook

[5] Sometimes Madala!

[6] Made of pasteboard for small specimens and wood for large.

[7] Barth's *Travels in Central Africa*. Vol. i, p. 370.

[8] Dr. Barth's *Travels in Central Africa*. Vol. i, p. 399.

[9] "ABISGEE," Hausa name; an evergreen, willow-like bush, which has a pungent skunk odour. It bears large clusters of currant-like fruit in June and July. This bush was found only in Aïr, and it may be *Boscia salicifolia, Oliver* (Capparidaceæ).

[10] The mountains of Baguezan, Timia, Agalak, Goundaï, Agarageur, Faodet, and Tamgak may be said to form almost one continuous range, whereas Aguellal is a detached mountain range.

[11] Described by Lord Rothschild

www.ingramcontent.com/pod-product-compliance
Lightning Source LLC
Chambersburg PA
CBHW071621170426
43195CB00038B/1590